THE HORSE CARE
HANDBOOK

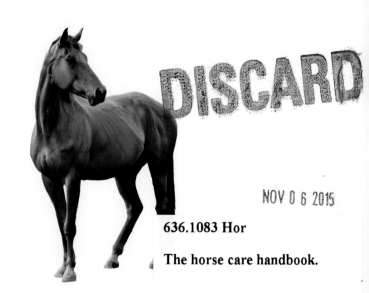

THE HORSE CARE
HANDBOOK

A COMPLETE INTRODUCTION
TO THE WORLD OF HORSES

Edited by Ashley Wood

CHARTWELL
BOOKS

A QUARTO BOOK

This edition published in 2015 by
CHARTWELL BOOKS
an imprint of Book Sales
a division of Quarto Publishing Group USA Inc.
142 West 36th Street, 4th Floor
New York, New York 10018
USA

ISBN 13: 978-0-7858-3345-1
QUAR.HOCA

Conceived, designed, and produced by
Quarto Publishing plc
The Old Brewery
6 Blundell Street
London N7 9BH

Senior editor: Ruth Patrick
Designer: Paul Griffin
Design assistant: Saffron Stocker
Picture researcher: Sarah Bell
Proofreader: Claire Waite Brown
Indexer: Ann Barrett

Art director: Caroline Guest
Creative director: Moira Clinch
Publisher: Paul Carslake

Manufactured in Singapore by Pica
  Digital International Pte Ltd.
Printed in China by Midas Printing
  International Ltd.

Contents

FOREWORD 6

ABOUT THE HORSE 8

EQUIPMENT 38

RIDING BASICS 92

COMPETITIVE RIDING 116

HORSE CARE 136

HORSE HEALTH 170

INDEX 188

ACKNOWLEDGMENTS 192

FOREWORD

All domestic horses are members of one animal species, *Equus caballus*, descended from the wild horses that once roamed central Asia.

The sole surviving subspecies of wild horse is Przewalski's horse, named for the Russian explorer who first described it in the late nineteenth century. It is related to the rhino and the tapir, has a false nostril in its nasal cavities, and walks on one toe.

The earliest mammal ancestors of the horse were the Condylarthra, 75 million years ago. They were about the size of a fox, had five toes on each limb, and lived in the swamps of the northern hemisphere. Eventually the swamps dried out and five toes, which had been an advantage in the swamps, became a disadvantage on the dry plains. Over millions of years the toes disappeared until *Pliohippus*, the first single-toed horse ancestor evolved, about 10 million years ago.

Early horses and man

Prehistoric man hunted primitive horses for meat and hides. The nomadic tribesmen of the steppes captured foals, taking them with them on their travels, and eventually breeding from them to provide milk, meat, hides, and transport. The first documented evidence of horses being ridden is that of migrating steppe warriors attacking China around 4,000 BCE.

The Norwegian Fjord and other wild ponies have changed little, but other horses were domesticated and selectively bred. In Europe large animals were required to carry knights; later these "cold bloods"—such as the Shire and Clydesdale—were used in farming. In the Middle East the Bedouin bred the fastest mares with the best endurance and the best looking stallions to create the Arab breed.

The Norwegian Fjord horse is almost unchanged since prehistoric times.

ABOUT THE HORSE

In this chapter you will learn how to recognize the parts of the horse's body, identify colors and markings, and measure your horse.

To improve your skill in handling your horse, there are sections on body language, vices, and horse whispering. There is also advice on the most critical decision you will face as a rider—the purchase of your first horse—and information on what pitfalls to avoid. It is essential to know what you can reasonably expect and what to look out for when you purchase an animal, to ensure you are happy with your horse.

The Dartmoor pony (left) has roamed the wilds of Dartmoor in Devon, England, for centuries—one was even named in the will of a Saxon bishop in 1012. It is a perfect child's first pony.

LESSON 1 | **Breeds of the horse**

On the following pages is a selection of the best known of over 350 horse breeds that exist in the world today.

American Quarter horse USA
The most popular breed in the United States, it is famous for its high speed over races of ¼ mile (0.6 km) and its tough, strong quarter and thighs.

American Saddlebred USA
This popular American breed with its three-and five-gaited paces is also used for pleasure riding, driving, and jumping.

Appaloosa USA
The spectacular coloring of this breed is most unusual and is not unlike the mottled skin of horses in prehistoric cave paintings.

Arab ARABIAN PENINSULA
The Arab is the oldest pure breed in the
world and has very distinctive features,
particularly the dished face and flaring
nostrils, and high, flowing tail carriage.

Clydesdale SCOTLAND
Clydesdales are still used for work on farms,
deliveries, showing, and breeding. They are
exported in large numbers to the United
States and other countries.

Friesian NETHERLANDS
This ancient black breed is extremely
popular for driving, has spectacular action,
and is sometimes used for circus displays.

Morgan USA
Descended from one very dominant stallion,
this highly popular breed is used for showing
and driving.

LESSON 1 | **Breeds of the horse** continued

Mustang USA
The unsung hero of just about every Western movie, the Mustang is the original horse of the Wild West. Tough and agile, its "cow sense" made it the ideal ranch animal.

New Forest pony ENGLAND
Horses have roamed free in the New Forest area since the eleventh century. These days, the New Forest is bred and exported worldwide for a variety of different uses.

Pony of the Americas USA
A new American breed developed from crossing a Shetland with an Appaloosa is now popular as a versatile riding mount.

Selle Français FRANCE
The Selle Français is one of the most highly sought after competition breeds in all Olympic disciplines.

Shetland SHETLAND ISLES
Although a children's favorite, the Shetland is the strongest horse for its size in the world and capable of carrying adults. It is the smallest of the nine British native breeds.

Shire ENGLAND
Shires are thought to have originated from Old English Black horses of the Middle Ages or the Great horses on which knights rode into battle.

Thoroughbred ENGLAND
This outstanding breed is fundamental to the sport of racing worldwide, both on the flat and over fences.

Trakehner GERMANY
The Trakehner is truer to type than any other warmblood. It makes an outstandingly successful sporthorse, excelling at Dressage and show jumping.

LESSON 2 | **Points of the horse**

The parts of a horse are called the "points"—this is specialist jargon, which has remained unchanged for centuries.

It is important not to confuse the points of the horse with a horse with black points—the former refers to the parts of a horse, and the latter is a horse with black legs, mane, and tail.

The terms used to describe different parts of the equine anatomy, and the names of many of the diseases that affect them, have evolved during thousands of years' close contact between humans and horses—and for that reason, the origin of many of these words is obscure. The derivation of some terms, such as "stifle" (the equine equivalent of the human knee joint), is lost in antiquity, but some of the words come from Medieval English (such as *fitlok* or *fetlak*: "fetlock"), or originate from Old English (such as *hōh*: "hock"); other terms have evolved through Old French, thus "pastern" comes from *pasturon*, the tether used to tie up horses around this part of their legs when at pasture.

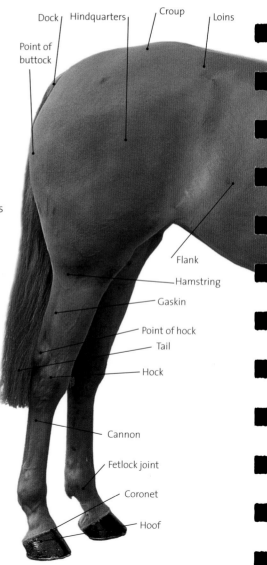

Dock
Hindquarters
Croup
Loins
Point of buttock
Flank
Hamstring
Gaskin
Point of hock
Tail
Hock
Cannon
Fetlock joint
Coronet
Hoof

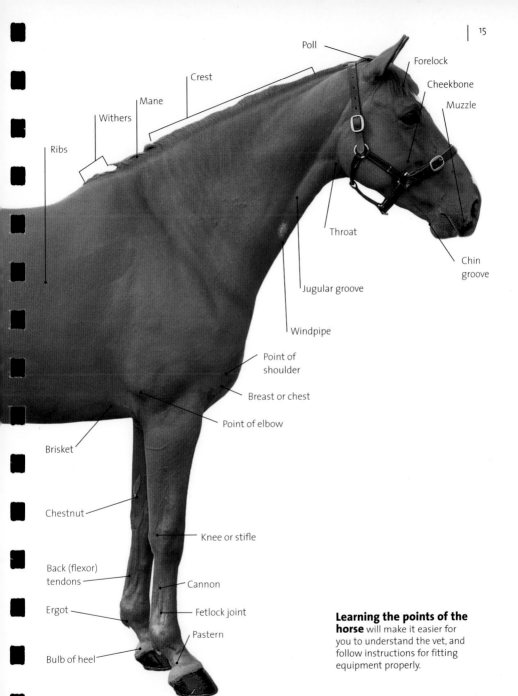

Poll

Crest

Mane

Withers

Ribs

Forelock

Cheekbone

Muzzle

Throat

Chin
groove

Jugular groove

Windpipe

Point of
shoulder

Breast or chest

Point of elbow

Brisket

Chestnut

Knee or stifle

Back (flexor)
tendons

Cannon

Ergot

Fetlock joint

Pastern

Bulb of heel

**Learning the points of the
horse** will make it easier for
you to understand the vet, and
follow instructions for fitting
equipment properly.

LESSON 2 | **Points of the horse** continued

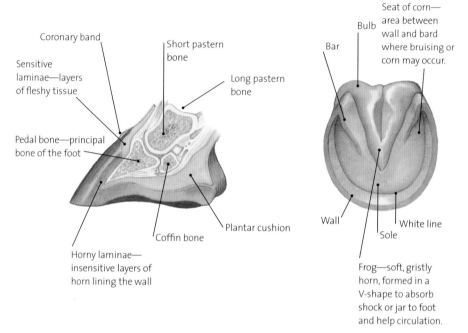

Coronary band

Sensitive laminae—layers of fleshy tissue

Short pastern bone

Long pastern bone

Pedal bone—principal bone of the foot

Horny laminae—insensitive layers of horn lining the wall

Coffin bone

Plantar cushion

Seat of corn—area between wall and bard where bruising or corn may occur.

Bulb

Bar

Wall

Sole

White line

Frog—soft, gristly horn, formed in a V-shape to absorb shock or jar to foot and help circulation.

You may find it easier to understand the hoof if you think about it in relation to your own foot. The horse essentially walks on the tip of its toe—with the toenail growing all around it and your ankle roughly approximating the horse's knee.

Horse respiration: interesting facts

- Horses are unable to breathe through their mouths.

- If the horse turns his head too far under it will struggle to breathe.

- When galloping, horses can only breathe in when their forelegs are extended.

- The oxygen uptake area in horses' lungs is 27,000 square feet (2,500 sq m). It is only 970 square feet (90 sq m) in humans.

Measuring the horse

The horse is measured to the withers—the point where
the neck meets the back. A measuring stick is placed
beside the horse next to its forelegs with the measure taken
horizontally across the highest point of the withers. Horses
are measured in "hands"—one hand is equal to the width
of an average hand of 4 inches (10 cm). A horse of 15 hands
is therefore 60 inches (150 cm) tall.

Horses are given a height only when fully mature, at six
years old, but young horses are given an estimated height
based on the height of their parents. Children often think
that ponies are baby horses, but in fact, a pony is a fully
mature horse smaller than 14.2 hands.

17hh

15hh

12hh

10hh

Who's the shortest? The
little Shetland pony is the
smallest of the group, coming
in at 10 hands high; next up in
size is the Pony of the Americas,
followed by the Saddlbred, then
the towering Shire horse.

LESSON 3 | **Colors and markings**

There is a vast range of horse colors in existence—
this is a simple guide to some of them.

Most common colors

Bay Body color ranging from light to dark brown with black mane, tail, and legs.

Strawberry roan A coat with white hairs evenly mixed through the base color.

Chestnut A reddish body color with no black and a mane and tail the same color or lighter.

Brown Body color ranging from light to dark brown with no black hairs present.

Blue roan As for strawberry roan (above) but the base color is gray/blue.

Liver chestnut As for chestnut (above) but both mane and tail are darker in color.

Less common colors

Palomino A golden coat with a white mane and tail. It is obtained by mating a chestnut with a cream horse, and does not breed true.

Odd colored Spotting pattern of white and two other colors.

A Pinto horse has multicolored patches of white, brown, and/or black (known outside the United States as piebald, skewbald, and odd colored). In the United States these are classed as Paint horses if they have Quarter horse or Thoroughbred bloodlines.

Yellow dun Yellowish coat with primitive markings: a black stripe along the spine, a black mane and tail, and possibly faint stripes on the legs.

Black For a horse to be true black, it must be black except for white markings. The hairs around the muzzle and eyes must also be black.

Cream A pink-skinned horse with pale cream hairs and pale eyes.

Fleabitten gray A white-haired horse that has red hairs flecked throughout the coat.

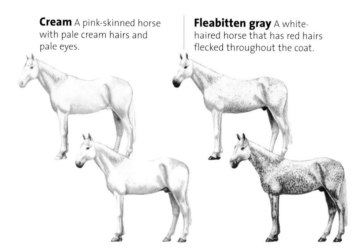

Gray A horse with black skin and white coat or a mixture of white and black hairs.

Dapple gray A dark-colored horse with lighter rings of graying hairs throughout.

LESSON 3 | **Colors and markings** continued

White markings

Horses of any color can have white markings on their faces and legs. Some breeds have specific markings associated with them. The Clydesdale is distinguishable from the Shire by its white legs, extending over the knees and up to a pale-colored belly. White leg markings on Show and Dressage horses are desirable as they emphasize the horses' action.

White face
White extends to or past the eyes. Eyes may be blue.

Stripe Narrow white strip down the middle of the face.

Blaze Wide stripe down the center of the face, not extending to the eyes.

Star White marking between or above the eyes. Can combine with other facial markings.

Snip White marking on the muzzle between the nostrils.

LESSON 4 |
Horse passports

In addition to the sex, height, age, breed, and coat color, horses' markings are also recorded on veterinary certificates to help identify them.

A drawing and a written description of the face and leg markings are used. Exact descriptions of limb markings, such as "white to mid-cannon" are now used, rather than the previous vague terms such as "socks" or "stockings."

The veterinary certificate, breed registration documentation, and travel passport all need to be kept in a safe place—some livery stables will require copies, and correct documentation may also be necessary for competing. Check competition rules and if in doubt ask your vet.

Leg markings
The terminology used to describe leg markings used to be vague (see right), but is now more precise. Below left is a white coronet and below right is a white to knee.

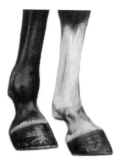

LESSON 5 | **The paces**

The horse has four basic paces or gaits: walk, trot, canter, and gallop.

There are variations within these paces, which demonstrate collection or extension (smaller and larger strides).

The walk, the slowest gait, is a four-beat gait with the animal picking up each leg independently of the other. The four beats should be even and regular at all times and there should be no stiffness.

The trot is a two-beat gait on alternate diagonal legs with a moment of suspension in between. It should be free and active with regular steps.

The canter is a three-beat gait and can be an extremely comfortable pace. It is the most important pace to perfect for jumping, as from a controlled, even canter the horse is able to jump out of its stride.

The gallop is a speeded-up version of the canter. This makes the four-movement sequence much more difficult to see when all the weight is on the off foreleg.

Some breeds also have unusual gaits. The Pace is a two-time movement like the trot, but unlike the trot, both legs on one side move together. It is uncomfortable to ride at speed, but faster than a trot.

The ambling gaits, including the running walk and the rack, are four-beat movements at a speed somewhere between a walk and a canter. They are perfect for trail and long distance riding as they are faster than a walk, can be kept up for a long time, and are very comfortable for the rider.

SEE ALSO
European—riding the paces **page 98**
Western—riding the paces **page 104**

Walk—a pace in four time.

Trot—a pace in two time.

The trot is one of the four paces of the horse—with practice it can be extended and collected (see page 121).

Canter—a pace in three time.

Gallop—a pace in four time.

LESSON 6 | **Body language**

Back off! The chestnut horse in this picture is warning the bay away from its food—if your horse is pulling this face at you, it's safe to say it is agitated. Be careful, as a warning nip or kick that might not cause serious injury to another horse may be considerably more painful to you.

In the wild, horses use body language to communicate with the rest of the herd.

If you take the time to study their behavior you will be better able to understand your own horse. This may be very important; if your horse begins to act out of character there is usually an underlying reason.

Signs to watch for

The stance of the horse is very informative; it may hold a leg up in pain or point out a front one to relieve pressure. Many rest a hind leg, but this does not necessarily mean they are uncomfortable—horses can sleep standing up, and often rest a leg while doing so.

A horse that is stressed will tense—causing its head to be raised, and steps to become short and quick. The horse's nostrils and eyes may be wider than usual. It may clench its tail between its legs, or swish it around. Each of these taken in isolation may be perfectly innocent, but more than one could mean a horse is in pain or frightened.

Hanging head A tired horse looks rather listless and sleepy, and its eyes are periodically closing. It might hang its head, rest a leg, or even lie down (horses only lie down if exhausted or feeling secure).

Flat ears and wrinkled nose This unhappy horse frequently flattens its ears back and occasionally wrinkles its nose. Try to work out what is causing the problem or vary the horse's day with a spell in the paddock or a change in routine.

Wide eyes A white-eyed, frightened horse will tense its muscles away from scary sights and sounds. Its instinct is to run, and if unable to run, to fight. Be positive and talk calmly—if the horse thinks you are afraid it will be more frightened.

Ears flattened in anger An angry horse flattens its ears back in a menacing attitude and will snake its head low, open its eyes wide, and bare its teeth before attacking. It may swing its quarters toward you, or even kick out.

Alert pose Something strange has caught this horse's eye. Its head is raised and alert, and its ear flicks suspiciously. A horse that does not react at all to sounds or movements is likely to have something wrong.

Ear flicks with wide eyes This suspicious horse is flicking its ears and showing the white of its eye. If it thinks there is something threatening it is likely to run—in the wild, the suspicious sound might be a predator.

LESSON 7 | Horse whisperers

The most significant development in equestrianism since the early 1980s has been the rise of the horse whisperers, who have a new way of perceiving horses based on the modern use of the horse—that of companion and friend.

Horse whisperers emphasize gentle, nonviolent training techniques and urge riders to understand and empathize with their horses. They use elements of the horse's wild behavior (such as its herd instincts and hierarchical social structure) to explain the success of their training.

As yet, no horse has been trained to Olympic standard using only the whisperer method—but it is spreading fast among those who own their own horses, and ride purely for pleasure.

One of the best examples of the whisperer's approach is the story of Shy Boy. This was a wild Mustang that Monty Roberts—trainer and world-famous horse whisperer—tamed with his "Join-Up" method. The horse was habituated to saddle, bridle, and rider and became a useful mount.

After several months Monty decided to test the bond between himself and the horse and he released it back into the herd. It stayed with the herd for one night but returned to him in the morning.

Monty explains, "All by himself Shy Boy exhibited his true freedom and chose to come home."

SEE ALSO
Body language **page 24**

Horses are highly intelligent animals with a complex social system; by learning their language, it is possible to bond closely with them.

LESSON 8 | **Behavioral science**

By studying how your horse sees the world and how it thinks, you will be able to better understand the things it does, and prevent problems.

Horses are entirely different to people: they are prey animals; humans are predators. Our bodies are designed differently because of this—the horse is designed to run away from danger, at high speed and for a long time.

This racehorse has blinkers to prevent it being distracted by horses on either side.

How your horse sees the world

Horses have prominent eyes on the side of the skull. This enables them to detect predators while they are grazing. Horses have two blind spots: directly behind them, and under their nose. The sensitive hairs around the muzzle are important for finding food and water. Horses have a very limited field of binocular vision, and have difficulty in judging distances when the obstacle is not straight ahead.

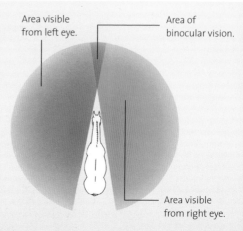

Area visible from left eye.

Area of binocular vision.

Area visible from right eye.

Turning the head When a horse sees something unfamiliar it will turn its head to see it more clearly. This is because it can only judge distance and depth with the small area of binocular vision directly in front.

Throwing the head A horse's eyes are prominent and prone to injury. When the horse sees something it does not recognize, it will throw its head up to protect them, and jump away from the frightening object, in case it is a predator.

Kicking or bolting The horse cannot see directly behind—a sudden sound from behind, or a slap on the quarters, is likely to be answered by a kick or bolt. When grooming your horse, keep one hand on it at all times, and if you have a nervous horse talk to it so it can tell where you are.

Protecting the hooves A lame horse is easy prey to any predator, and for this reason horses are very nervous of changing surfaces. This may cause problems when loading, or riding on a road—your horse may perceive mends in the road as holes.

Claustrophobia Horses rely on speed to escape predators, so enclosed spaces may frighten them. A horse kept in its stable for too long will develop vices (see page 30). An open window or a rope across the door may help relieve claustrophobia.

Herd instinct Horses are herd animals and become stressed when kept alone. If they are unable to befriend other horses some will form a bond with other animals—goats, rabbits, or stable cats have been known.

LESSON 9 | **Common vices**

Nearly all vices develop in stabled horses as a result of boredom.

A horse's natural habitat is wide-open spaces, and no matter how large the stall, horses do not like being confined for long periods without exercise. Turning a horse out to pasture usually stops boredom and cures many vices. However, bad habits such as wood chewing and cribbing can persist in pasture, and may be copied by other horses.

Preventing vices Preventing vices is largely a case of preventing boredom and stress. Putting horses in larger barns, providing companion animals, and increasing exercise may all help. Turning a horse out every day alleviates boredom, provides rest, and allows the horse to live in a natural state. Turning out for a few weeks may even give a horse time to forget a vice that has just started.

Crib biting A horse that grabs hold of things with its teeth—especially the tops of stable doors—is called a crib biter. This can lead to windsucking, where the horse gulps in air as it grabs the top of the door, which can cause colic (see page 183). A cribbing strap can help discourage windsucking.

Chewing This horse is wearing a bib to prevent it chewing its blanket, which can become very expensive if too many blankets get ruined. A bib can also be helpful to stop the horse chewing bandages, such as those holding a dressing in place.

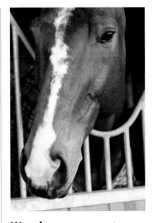

Stall walking Stall-walking horses are restless and constantly move around in the stable. It affects horses that have been cooped up in their stalls for long periods. Some are content to be tied up when stressed—giving them a hay net may help to occupy their minds, and others like music or toys.

Pawing Pawing tends to wear out shoes unevenly and increase farrier bills. Horses paw for a number of reasons—it could be the onset of stall walking or it could be just impatience or greediness. Pawing could be a sign of pain, or the horse may simply be curious. A sharp "no" every time the horse paws may help.

Weaving Weaving is where the horse rocks from side to side, weaving its head from left to right. An anti-weaving grill is the most effective way to stop the practice. Hanging toys from the top of the door or inside the stable can help to alleviate the problem.

LESSON 10 | **Buying a horse**

Before considering buying a horse or pony, it is essential to ensure that you really can cope with owning one.

Choosing the right horse

The size and shape of rider and horse will play a key role. Heavy people require strong horses of a hunter or cob type. Below is a general guide, but much depends on skill and experience.

- **12.2 hands (127 cm): average children of 12 years old or under.**

- **13.2–14.2 hands (137–147 cm): average children of 14 to 16 years.**

- **14.2–15.2 hands (147–157 cm): average children of 16 to 18 years or adults.**

- **15.2 hands (157 cm) and over: suitable for competent riders of all ages.**

Horses are both time-consuming and expensive, but, if you are prepared to put in the necessary hard work, they make wonderful companions and are a joy to own.

Choose a horse that is suitable in temperament, height, and type for you. If you are inexperienced go for a calm, well-schooled animal that is confident and happy in its work, and easily controlled—an experienced, sensible horse that will get you going and give you confidence. This is often advertised as a "schoolmaster."

Remember: if you are choosing a horse that needs to be a specific height for a certain activity, have it measured or see its height certificate before deciding to buy. For specific information and advice on buying a horse, turn to the next page.

SEE ALSO
Points of the horse **page 14**
Colors and markings **page 18**
Common vices **page 30**
Stabling **page 40**

Owning horses
is hard work, but
very rewarding.

LESSON 10 | **Buying a horse** continued

Buying checklist

It is essential to know the pitfalls when buying a horse. Make sure you ask plenty of questions and never get drawn into something you do not feel confident about.

- Take a knowledgeable friend.
- Make a list of questions to ask about size, color, sex, temperament, and the aspects of riding you are interested in.
- Ask the owners if the horse or pony is quiet in traffic, with children, dogs, other animals, etc.
- Why are they selling? Do their reasons seem genuine to you?
- Watch the horse being groomed and tacked up.
- Watch the owner riding the horse before trying it yourself—you will be able to see its gaits better, and are less likely to be injured.

- Try the horse in an enclosed area, on open grass, and, if possible, on the road.
- If you plan to compete, try loading the horse yourself.
- If the horse has a stable name, think carefully about what it implies... Fidget is not a good sign!
- Always get the horse vetted to ensure it is sound in eye, wind, heart, and limb.
- Phone back later to give yourself time to think before making a final decision.

Choosing the right horse (right) will allow you to form a strong partnership.

Buying a young horse (left) must be carefully thought through—breaking in should be professionally done.

Where to find a horse

Reputable dealers—tell them what you want, what you hope to do with the animal, and how experienced you are.

Friends may well know of a pony that is outgrown or no longer required. Check carefully what work the pony has done before.

"For Sale" pages in horse magazines and local papers. Phone first with questions and write down the responses, then check someone will ride the horse for you.

Auction sales—not recommended for the first-time buyer because of the difficulty in trying out horses.

Two's company
Horses are happier in company—
where possible, always keep horses in
pairs. Horse charities often have suitable
companion animals.

EQUIPMENT

Equipment in the stable is not confined to the horse's box. It also involves tack, rugs, bandages, grooming equipment, and riding gear. In this chapter, all of these topics are covered in separate sections, after a discussion of the stabling and paddock requirements essential for a happy horse.

Horse equipment is not cheap, so each purchase must be considered carefully and subsequently cared for. Each section covers the benefits of different types of equipment, how to purchase it, and how to care for it.

Stable equipment comes in all kinds of colors, materials, and styles—research the options before you buy.

LESSON 11 | **Stabling**

The stable needs to be safe, sheltered, and well sited to make it as easy to manage as possible.

Running water and storage space for feed and bedding are just the basics, as is an area set out for the muck heap. This needs to be far away enough to reduce the smell and flies, without becoming a major trek every time you clean out the stall or stable.

In standing stalls horses are unable to move around, so they are only suitable for horses that are stabled for short periods—at riding schools, for example.

SEE ALSO
Livery **page 43**
Bedding **page 44**
Pasture **page 46**
Safety and security **page 48**

Stabling essentials

- **Tack room** should be easily accessible and big enough for all your equipment. Use bridle hooks and saddle racks to store tack off the floor. Rugs will also need to be stored.

- **Feed stores** pose a fire risk; hay is best kept with bedding separately for this reason. Grains and feed buckets can be kept closer to the stables. Grain bins must be vermin proof, and inaccessible to loose horses.

- **Access** must be available for delivering bedding and fodder and removing muck, and also to suitable areas for riding out.

- **New stables** should face south, for warmth, and be in a sheltered position. In the United States, regulations regarding new stables vary from state to state.

- **Stall size** is directly related to the size of the horse. A good size for a stable is 14 x 12 feet (4.5 x 3.5 m), with a height of 10 feet (3 m).

- **Flooring** of sand or dirt must drain well; concrete floors with rubber matting must have a slight slope and shallow gutter.

- **Stall doors** must be at least 4 x 8 feet (1.5 x 2.5 m). They should be divided in half for ventilation. The horse must be unable to get over it, but able to look out. External doors should have an overhang of 3 feet (1 m) to prevent rain blowing in.

- **Electric light sockets** should have a protective cover to prevent hay from touching a hot bulb. Cables must be horse proof, as must the waterproof light switch.

The "barn" system is common in the United States; box stalls facing over a central walkway and tack and feed rooms enclosed against weather. This works well, with adequate ventilation.

A stable yard consists of a single row of buildings incorporating stables, tack room, and feed room side by side. This is the most typical stabling arrangement in the UK.

LESSON 11 | **Stabling**   continued

The diagram below shows two loosebox-style
stables side-by-side, the one on the left showing
the ideal external features and the one on the
right showing the internal features.

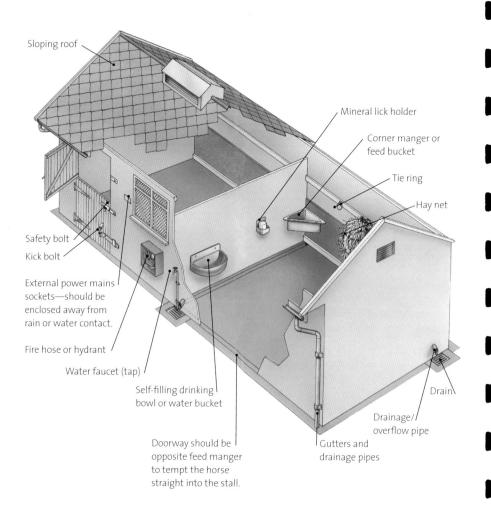

Sloping roof

Mineral lick holder

Corner manger or
feed bucket

Tie ring

Hay net

Safety bolt

Kick bolt

External power mains
sockets—should be
enclosed away from
rain or water contact.

Fire hose or hydrant

Water faucet (tap)

Self-filling drinking
bowl or water bucket

Doorway should be
opposite feed manger
to tempt the horse
straight into the stall.

Gutters and
drainage pipes

Drainage/
overflow pipe

Drain

LESSON 12 | **Livery**

If you do not have your own land,
you can keep your horse at a boarding
stable (at livery).

A boarding stable—offering either full board or a do-it-yourself arrangement—will also help if you have other time commitments.

Full board means you will be paying someone else to look after your horse full time. The horse will even be exercised and turned out into a paddock area for you by the staff during the week and those times when you are unable to do so yourself. The expense varies according to the individual arrangement you have with the owners of the facility.

Do-it-yourself means you literally pay for the rental of a box stall and the use of a paddock and look after your own horse. This service is often offered by riding stables—which can be convenient for regular schooling. Your horse is likely to be fed by other people in both establishments, so you should display its feed chart prominently. Keep it up to date with any changes, and let everyone know if your horse is on medication (and whether any side effects are likely).

SEE ALSO
Stabling **page 40**
Pasture **page 46**
Safety and security **page 48**

Keeping your horse at a livery stable
will give both of you the chance to make
new friends.

LESSON 13 | **Bedding**

Bedding is necessary to allow a stabled horse to lie down and rest in comfort.

Bedding also prevents the horse's feet from being jarred on a hard floor and encourages it to urinate.

A wide variety of materials can be used, either fresh (changed at least once daily) or as a deep litter that may not need changing for months at a time.

Cleanliness is an absolute essential throughout the yard, but nowhere more so than in the stall or stable itself. Some types of bedding make this easier to achieve than others, but it's often a matter of personal preference or even a case of what is readily available in your area. Straw, wood shavings, and rubber sheeting are the main types used, although paper and peat are possible alternatives.

Straw is an ideal bedding material because it is easy to clear out and relatively inexpensive.

SEE ALSO
Mucking out **page 138**
Heel bug **page 177**
Thrush **page 179**

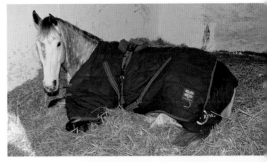

Clean bedding will prevent you needing to spot wash stable stains on pale-colored horses.

Straw is commonly used in some stables, and is easy to clear out. Ensure it is of good quality and not moldy. Wheat straw is preferable, because horses tend to eat barley and oat straw. Many horses are allergic to the dust and molds in straw.

Wood shavings are light and easy to work with, and useful for horses that eat straw or have allergies. If plastic wrapped, it has the advantage of being able to be stored outside. The only disadvantage is that it can be difficult to dispose of because it takes a long time to rot down.

Peat moss absorbs moisture and odors really well, and lasts longer as deep litter bedding. Horses cannot eat peat and as it is so dry they are less likely to get thrush. In addition, it makes great fertilizer!

Deep litter is less daily work. Remove fresh droppings and damp patches, add new bedding then rake over. At a depth of 1 foot (30 cm) clean out completely. Deep litter beds are warm but produce many fungal spores.

Wood shavings are a good alternative to hay if your horse suffers from allergies.

LESSON 14 | **Pasture**

A horse's pasture should be safe and secure, with adequate grazing, a fresh water supply, and some shelter. Permanent pasture is best for horses; they like established grasses and deep-rooted weeds.

You will need a minimum of 1 acre (0.4 ha) per horse; it is best not to keep too many in a small area because it encourages worms. Grazing should be divided in two, and each half grazed alternately.

Fencing should be 4 feet (1.5 m) high to discourage escapists. Post-and-rail fencing or a healthy hedge is the best fence—a horse will quickly find any weak spots and push its way to freedom. Barbed wire or spike wooden paling fences can result in appalling injuries, and wire netting is not sufficiently strong to contain horses.

Pasture gates must be strong and securely latched. Ideally, they should not be situated in a corner of the field, since this can lead to animals being cornered and bullied when being turned out.

Horses or ponies in pasture all through the winter need some form of shelter to give them protection from the weather. A shelter should be at least as large as a box stall for a horse, and preferably a little larger; it should be open on the side facing away from the prevailing wind. A hard floor is essential, because a horse cannot rest when standing in cold mud.

SEE ALSO
Safety and security **page 48**
Feeds and feeding **page 142**
Winter care **page 154**
Common ailments **page 176**

Horses need to graze and move around freely in order to keep mentally and physically healthy.

LESSON 15 | **Safety and security**

Fire is one of the main hazards at a stable; there should be a strict "no smoking" policy and regular checks of all electrical appliances and wiring.

Barns and grounds should be kept free of junk, cans, and bottles, which can ignite in direct sunlight, and fire extinguishers must be readily available.

All fencing should be regularly checked to ensure it is safe and stock-proof, and gates onto roads should be padlocked. Security lighting may be a sensible precaution, and regular checks on the yard cannot be overemphasized. All tack rooms need to be very secure and the contents realistically insured and cataloged.

Ensure your horse is identifiable in case of theft. Precautions include branding, microchip implants, lip tattoos, and hoofbrands. Take photographs of your horse showing both sides and markings or scars; keep these in a file with your vaccination card, registration papers, and health records.

Freeze or heat branding
makes your horse less
attractive to thieves.

Secure fencing is essential to
prevent injury, escape, and theft.

TACK ESSENTIALS

In this section, the more popular types of saddles and bridles and their uses are discussed. Other tack items, such as bandages, rugs, and numnahs, are also covered.

LESSON 16 | **Buying tack**

Good quality tack and equipment are essential for the safety of you and your horse, so always buy the best that you can afford. Treat your tack well and it will repay you with years of faithful service.

Well-maintained and correctly fitting tack adds to the overall look of your horse, whether you are riding out or in competition, so it is worth choosing items that look good on your horse.

A reputable saddler will tell you what you require, will professionally fit tack to your horse, and will give advice on looking after your equipment. This is even more important for inexperienced owners, or oddly shaped horses.

Ensure that the tack you buy is comfortable for both you and the horse and suitable for what you intend to do. The saddle in particular is a very personal item since it molds to the rider's shape and increases in comfort with age.

The use of secondhand saddlery depends on the quality and state of the items. Have everything carefully checked by a saddler. Make sure saddle trees are not broken and check all buckles and fastenings for excessive wear and tear. If tack has been well cared for, it should last for many years.

It is worth going to a professional barn or yard to see what tack and equipment is really necessary before investing in too many gimmicks. Watch the people working there as they "tack up" to learn how to use all tack correctly.

Specialist Dressage tack is required; this is often made to measure, so that the buckles line up under the eye.

SEE ALSO
Saddles **page 52**
Saddle extras **page 54**
Nosebands, bits, and bridles **page 56**
Western saddles **page 60**
Western bridles **page 62**
Horse rugs **page 68**
Boots and bandages **page 72**

LESSON 17 | **Saddles**

A correctly fitted saddle is an essential—an ill-fitting saddle will not only be painful for a horse, but can lead to permanent damage. It should be comfortable for the rider, and suitable for its intended use.

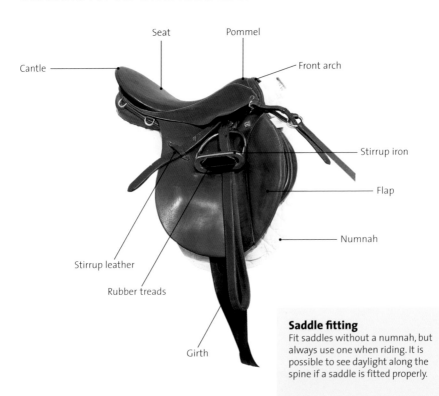

Seat

Pommel

Cantle

Front arch

Stirrup iron

Flap

Numnah

Stirrup leather

Rubber treads

Girth

Saddle fitting

Fit saddles without a numnah, but always use one when riding. It is possible to see daylight along the spine if a saddle is fitted properly.

General saddle

A general-purpose saddle can be used for all kinds of riding, but it will not be comfortable for long periods of specialist riding, and will not help you get the most out of your horse in competition.

Dressage saddle

The Dressage saddle is designed to allow the rider to sit deep in the saddle with long stirrups to allow greater control with smaller aids. The breadth and padding protects the horse's back from the large amount of sitting trot necessary.

Jump saddle

A jumping saddle has padded flaps, cut farther forward than in most saddles. This allows for the knee to fit snugly against the saddle when the stirrup leathers are shortened. The deep seat helps keep the rider's seat and weight situated in the deepest part of the saddle.

SEE ALSO
Saddle extras **page 54**
Western saddles **page 60**

LESSON 18 | **Saddle extras**

The saddle has many extras; all should be in good condition and well fitted.

The girth holds the saddle in place. Leather girths are strong, long-lasting, and easy to clean. Nylon makes a good easy-to-clean general-purpose girth. String girths are good for unclipped horses. A sheepskin sleeve is sometimes put around a girth as an extra protection against girth galls (see page 180).

The stirrup leathers should be a suitable size for the rider and adjustable in length. There are three main types of stirrup iron (see opposite), and the leather breastplate prevents the saddle from slipping back.

The other important saddle extras are described on these pages.

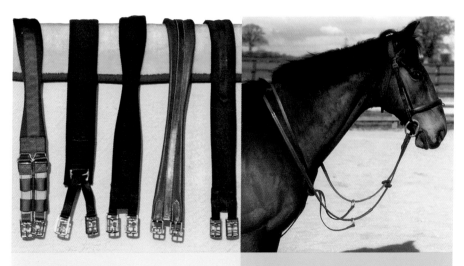

A variety of girths, some with elasticated inserts for extra "give."

The running martingale prevents the horse from putting his head up too high and out of the angle of control, helping to control and steer the horse.

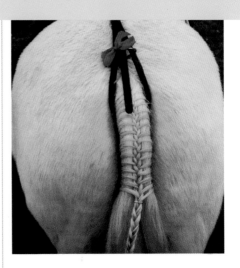

The numnah is used to soften the contact between saddle and horse, and to protect the leather. Left to right: felt; quilted cotton; foam-filled cotton; synthetic fur; real sheepskin.

The crupper stops the saddle slipping forward and does not cause discomfort. The red bow shows the horse may kick.

Safety stirrups have a rubber band that pulls off in a fall to prevent the rider being dragged along the ground. These are ideal for children.

Stirrups without tread have a gap for the tread on the rider's boot.

Stirrups with rubber treads prevent the foot slipping.

LESSON 19 | **Nosebands, bits, and bridles**

Choose a noseband and bridle that complements your horse's appearance. Choose a bit based on your horse's temperament, and check that you can adjust the bridle in case you use a different bit.

Nosebands

Grakle Cross-over noseband to prevent the horse crossing his jaw.

Flash Bottom strap fastens below the bit, preventing the mouth opening too wide.

Plain cavesson Most common noseband, sitting just below the cheekbones.

Drop noseband High on the nose, but fastened below the bit.

SEE ALSO
Western bridles **page 62**

Bridles

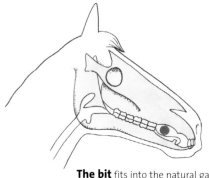

The bit fits into the natural gap between the horse's front and back teeth.

Bits

Loose-ring snaffle Constant slight movement prevents the horse from leaning on the bit.

Eggbutt snaffle One of the simplest and kindest bits.

Kimblewick curb Chain fastened around the chin groove to give extra control.

The double-bridle is required for advanced Dressage and has two sets of reins attached to two bits in the horse's mouth. One is a snaffle and the other a curb.

The hackamore is a bitless bridle using pressure on the sensitive nose to control horses with injured mouths.

LESSON 20 | **Tacking up**

Prepare to tack up by tying up the horse, brushing saddle and girth area, and picking out the hooves. The saddle should have the girths attached to the offside (right) and the stirrups run up.

Saddling

1 From the near (left) side, place the numnah and then the saddle over the horse's withers and slide it back into position. Never pull the saddle forward since this causes saddle rubs.

2 Lift numnahs up to the front arch of the saddle, so there is no pressure on the withers. Drop the girths gently down the offside, bend down, and pick up the girth when it stops swinging.

3 Do up the girth and straighten the flaps. Do not tighten until you are ready to mount—some horses breathe in as they are saddled to get extra slack!

SEE ALSO
Saddles **page 52**
Nosebands, bits, and
  bridles **page 56**

Bridling

Take the bridle with the throatlatch and noseband undone in your left hand and go to the near side of the horse. Place the reins over the horse's head and unfasten the halter.

1 With the right hand holding the bridle, lift the bit toward his mouth. Slip your fingers gently between the lips at the side, to ask him to open his mouth.

2 Slide the bridle up and slip one ear at a time through the headpiece. Straighten the browband.

3 Fasten the throatlatch and noseband. Check the bridle is fitted correctly between the cheekbones and lips so as not to cause soreness.

Untacking

Keep control of the horse by taking the reins over his head and onto your arm, or by buckling a halter around his neck.

1 Undo the noseband and throatlatch. Ease the bridle off over each ear by the headpiece. Gently lower the bridle until the horse lets go of the bit.

2 Run the stirrup irons up the leathers. Undo the girth. Lift the saddle at the pommel and slide it toward you; catch the girth and place it over the seat.

LESSON 21 | **Western saddles**

The most important item for the Western rider is the saddle; it is comfortable enough to spend days at a time in the saddle, and has a pommel made into a horn for roping cattle.

Either one or two cinches (girths) hold it in place over several blankets, and the weight is spread evenly over the horse's back. The stirrups must be broad and flat with wide fenders (stirrup leathers) for the long leg position. Many saddles have beautifully embossed leatherwork, especially those used for Western pleasure classes.

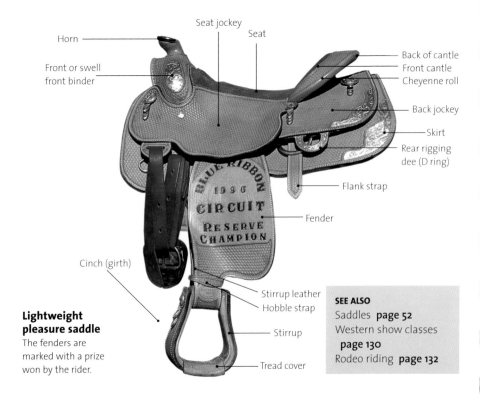

Horn

Front or swell front binder

Seat jockey

Seat

Back of cantle

Front cantle

Cheyenne roll

Back jockey

Skirt

Rear rigging dee (D ring)

Flank strap

Fender

Cinch (girth)

Stirrup leather

Hobble strap

Stirrup

Tread cover

Lightweight pleasure saddle
The fenders are marked with a prize won by the rider.

SEE ALSO
Saddles **page 52**
Western show classes
    page 130
Rodeo riding **page 132**

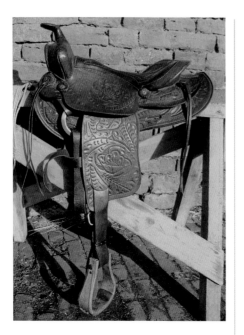

A lightweight barrel racing saddle; straight fenders twist the rider's feet inward, so they are soaked before use to shape them to fit the leg.

A modern Californian saddle with tapaderos (stirrup covers) to protect the feet from undergrowth; these can be lined with sheepskin in the winter.

Brightly colored blankets are traditionally used with Western saddles—cowboys used to sleep wrapped in them after a hard day's riding.

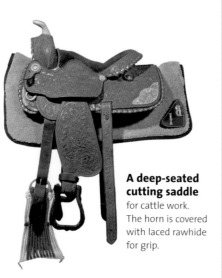

A deep-seated cutting saddle for cattle work. The horn is covered with laced rawhide for grip.

LESSON 22 | **Western bridles**

The Western bridle has no noseband and is designed for ease of putting on and comfort.

Usually, the bit is of a curb design, so extreme lightness of the hand is essential—Western reins are generally held in a loose curve, unlike the constant contact in European riding. In early training, often a conventional bridle and snaffle bit are used until the horse is ready for more advanced work.

The bosal is a simple thick noseband made of rawhide, finished with a knot at the back of the jaw attached to a plain headstall. A well-trained horse and skilled rider can make sudden stops, pivot, and turn at high speed while remaining perfectly balanced.

SEE ALSO
Nosebands, bits, and bridles **page 56**

The one-eared bridle shown here has a loop for one of the ears instead of a browband—an even simpler bridle has only a slit in the leather of the headstall for both ears.

The Californian style of reins is shown, the end of which can be used as a whip. The attractive gear shown here is suitable for the show ring.

A slip-eared bridle has a sliding headpiece; these are often shaped and decorated to enhance the horse's features.

In the Texan style, the reins are split into two—these can be held in both hands, or in one, depending on the level of training. The tack shown here is much more workmanlike.

LESSON 23 | **Western tacking up**

Saddle

A Western saddle is similar to any other saddle, but it is usually heavier. Before tacking up, make sure you tie up the horse and brush the back and girth area, and pick out the hooves.

1 If tacking up a tall horse, you may need quite a swing to get the saddle up onto the horse's back. Make sure the blankets are straight, flat, and central. Drop the cinch (girth) down on the other side (it should be attached to a leather strap on the offside).

2 Pick up the cinch and make sure it is not twisted, then feed the long leather strap through the cinch loop, then back through the D-ring.

SEE ALSO
Western saddles **page 60**
Western bridles **page 62**

3 Put several loops through the cinch and D-ring, then pull tight and either fasten with a buckle or tie in a knot.

4 Once the cinch is fully tightened, the end is tucked through the top tie holder and the fender (stirrup leather) is dropped back into position ready for mounting.

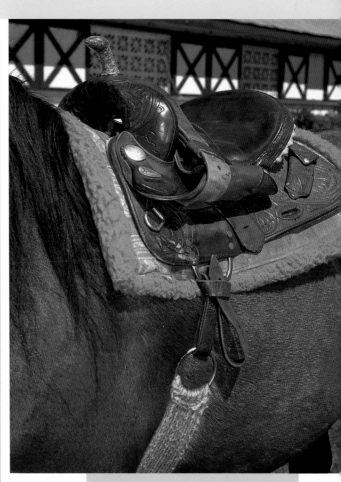

This workmanlike saddle has been secured with a shorter tie and a knot. The ring on the cinch is smooth and rounded, but care must be taken to ensure the skin does not pucker.

LESSON 23 | **Western tacking up** continued

Australian tack

Australian tack is very plain, like European tack, but comfortable and workmanlike in the style of Western tack, originally designed for traveling long distances in the outback. The second horse has the rider's gear strapped to it—the comfortable saddle will spread the weight evenly.

Bridle

All three types of Western bridle are simple to put on. The most important thing about putting on any bridle is to be gentle and not pull at your horse's mouth or ears too much.

1 Draw the bridle up the front of the head until the bit is resting just below the teeth—most horses will open their mouths.

2 If necessary, insert fingers, between lips at the side to persuade the horse to open its mouth. Slip the ears through the headpiece one at a time. Straighten the browband if necessary.

3 The throatlatch should be tightened but left loose enough to allow a hand's width between it and the jaw. Keep the reins over your arm so they are not trodden on.

LESSON 24 | **Horse rugs**

Stabled horses need some form of rug to keep warm, depending on the weather and if they have been clipped.

Keeping your horse warm will help it to stay in good condition since it will not be using energy stores just to keep warm.

Fitting a rug

You must ensure that whatever rug you choose to use is fitted properly and has all the buckles or ties fastened securely. An ill-fitting rug or loose strap could cause the horse to get tangled up and fall badly.

To find out what size of rug your horse needs, measure it from the center of the chest, along its side to the back of the quarters. Measuring from just in front of the withers, along the spine to the top of the tail can be useful in finding a perfectly fitting rug.

Rugging up
With all the buckles on the rug undone, and the horse tied up, swing the rug up and over his back (you may need to fold it first). Do up the front buckles and slide the rug back into place; bring the surcingles under his stomach and do them up, ensuring they are crossed. Do up one of the leg straps then pass the other through this loop before doing it up.

SEE ALSO
Clipping **page 148**
Transportation **page 164**
Winter care **page 155**

Summer protection
This is a specialist summer itch rug, which prevents the horse being bitten by midges (see page 177).

LESSON 24 | **Horse rugs** continued

Stable rugs made of quilted material come in various thicknesses and can be put on under a New Zealand rug in the pasture. This rug has a tail flap for extra warmth.

Sheets are usually made of cotton or a cotton mix, and are suitable for summer wear. They can be worn under heavier rugs to keep them clean.

New Zealand rugs are used for horses kept outside in inclement weather. They are designed to be weatherproof and non-slip, and have a variety of harness leg straps to ensure they remain in place. Horses in pasture with blankets must be checked regularly in case of accidents.

A woolen rug, held on with crupper, surcingle, and breastplate, is smart and warm for traveling or, with a roller, for use in the stable.

Exercise sheets keep the quarters and loins of the horse warm after clipping. They are often used on racehorses, or on clipped horses being ridden in inclement weather.

Anti-sweat sheets made of mesh are designed to allow the horse to cool down without catching a chill. They can be used with other rugs on top to warm a horse quickly—this may be useful in cases of shock.

Under blankets are basic blankets without the durable outer layer. The diagram at left shows how to fold them correctly. After folding the blanket, put the stable rug on top, then fold back the triangular corner, and hold in place with a surcingle.

LESSON 25 | **Boots and bandages**

Boots and bandages are used to protect the legs when traveling and prevent injury when the horse is being ridden. Bandages also protect the tail when traveling and hold dressings in place over injuries.

Traveling boots

Knee caps and hock boots combined with elasticized bandages for traveling; these must be fitted properly, otherwise they may cause problems.

Injury prevention boots

Brushing boots prevent adjacent legs from striking one another and causing injuries (see page 181).

Padded hock boots for traveling—these are fastened with Velcro, and quick to put on.

Foreleg brushing boots with Velcro.

SEE ALSO
Clipping **page 148**
Fitness for competition **page 162**
Transportation **page 164**
First aid for horses **page 184**

Hindleg brushing boots with buckles.

Over-reach boots
prevent the horse from stepping on the back of his forefeet, and are a sensible precaution when jumping.

Bell boots can either be in one piece, or have Velcro fastenings.

Petal bell boots can flap noisily; the petals come off when struck, and can be replaced.

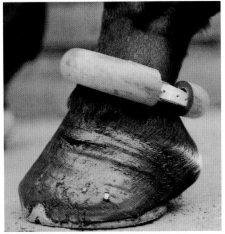

Brushing rings are basic, but effective in preventing injuries from the edges of the shoes (see page 180).

Fleece-lined tendon boots provide warmth, support, and protection.

LESSON 25 | **Boots and bandages** continued

Leg bandages

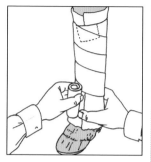

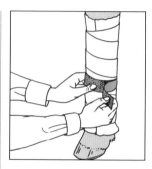

1 Place a bandage over leg wraps or other suitable padding.

2 Continue bandaging down over the fetlock joints.

3 Secure the end of the bandage with a knot or Velcro.

Tail bandages

Tail bandages are normally made of crêpe or stockinette; they are used to improve a horse's looks and also to protect the tail when traveling. Serious damage can result if tail bandages are put on too tight. They should never be left on overnight.

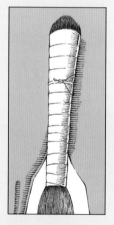

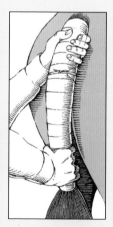

1 Gently lift the tail while quietly talking to the horse, and fold a bandage around under the tail from left to right.

2 Start at the top and work down in firm folds.

3 Carry on to the end of the dock, then back up. Secure with the tapes or Velcro on the bandage.

4 Bend the dock gently into shape if necessary as shown.

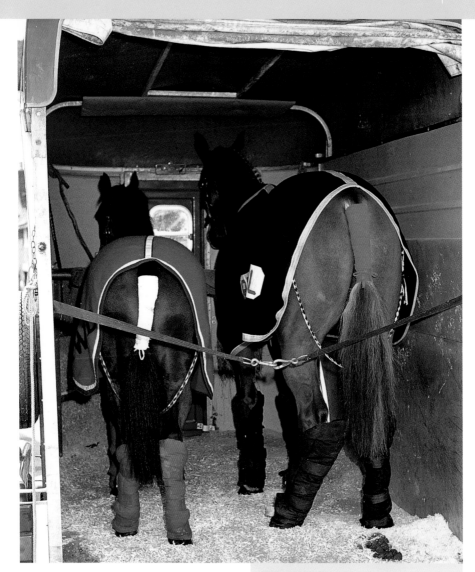

Horse travel wear
These horses are dressed for travel,
with rugs and a full set of bandages.
Partitions should always be used to
separate horses in transit.

LESSON 26 | **Cleaning tack**

All tack should be cleaned after use because tack kept in good condition will last for years.

Wipe down after use, and ensure all metal is kept dry. Never leave anything that is starting to unstitch or break, get it repaired by a saddler immediately.

Cleaning a bridle

1 Rinse the bit after every use and scrub with a brush; never use polish. Other metalwork should be cleaned with a damp cloth and dried. For shows, the bit rings, stirrup irons, buckles and metalwork can be buffed with metal polish.

2 Take the bridle to pieces at least once a week—the first time it might be a good idea to label the pieces so you can put it back together. Wipe off excessive mud with a damp cloth then use saddle soap to clean the leather.

3 Oil the leather if necessary—on the flesh (rough) side. You can remove mud from fiddly areas, such as laced reins, with a nailbrush.

CLEANING TACK | 77

Cleaning a saddle

1 Strip the saddle of its girth, girth guards, and stirrups—wipe off excessive mud with a damp cloth then check all the stitching, and areas where metal rests on the leather.

2 Soap the leather on both sides with saddle soap—if it foams, you have used too much water. The leather should be oiled to keep it supple; the saddle flaps need to be kept firm.

3 Polish the smooth side of the leather with a cloth to remove excess soap. Leather girths should be oiled to keep them supple—washable girths put in a bag, then put in the washing machine. Numnahs, halters, and rugs should also be kept clean—some launderettes will wash large horse rugs for you.

4 Where possible, put saddles on fence rails or stable doors—if neither is available, stand on the front arch with the girth tucked up to protect the pommel.

Carry the saddle by placing the front arch into the crook of your elbow.

RIDER ESSENTIALS

Rider turnout is very important for competing, and also for safety purposes during general riding. In this section the essentials for Western and European riding, and the clothing necessary for competing, are covered.

LESSON 27 |Riding gear

To begin riding, only basic safety gear is necessary—boots with a heel and a crash helmet are essentials, and riding schools may have spare helmets you can borrow. Later, you can buy a huge range of gear to suit your personality, and your interests.

Safety helmet

Shirt, sweater, or jacket

Gloves

Breeches

Chaps or boots

Safe, comfortable, and practical daily riding wear.

Safety helmet
Crash helmets come with or without integral peaks—you can fit a "silk" cover to those without peaks as shown here.

Long-sleeved top
Long sleeves will prevent scratches from hedges and trees, and from grazes when you fall off. It is wise to wear layers, and tops that undo all the way so you can take them off without removing your helmet. Never ride with flapping clothes.

SEE ALSO
The Pony Club and gymkhanas **page 118**
Dressage **page 120**
Show jumping **page 122**
Eventing **page 124**

Gloves

Riding gloves have dots of glue on the inner side so that you can grip the reins even in wet conditions. You may want a warmer pair for mucking out in the winter.

Jodhpurs

These come in a range of colors and fabrics and are usually skin-tight with padding on the inside of the knees. Jeans are not often worn in European riding, but are perfectly comfortable. In wet or cold conditions, a pair of tights worn underneath will lock in warmth.

Boots

Hunting boots are shown below, but jodhpur boots or "muckers" (boots designed for riding and stable work) plus chaps are better for non-competition work.

Specialist riding wear

Serious riders will acquire extra pieces of equipment, depending on their interests. Each specialist sport has its own specific requirements, with particular regard to safety aspects. Once you are serious enough to need specialist equipment, get an experienced friend to accompany you to a good riding wear store to obtain your outfit.

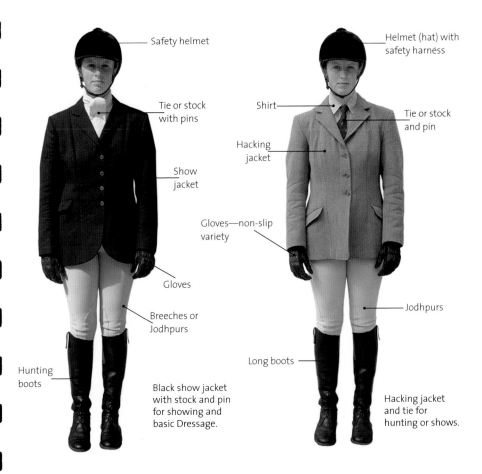

Safety helmet

Tie or stock with pins

Show jacket

Gloves

Breeches or Jodhpurs

Hunting boots

Black show jacket with stock and pin for showing and basic Dressage.

Helmet (hat) with safety harness

Shirt

Tie or stock and pin

Hacking jacket

Gloves—non-slip variety

Jodhpurs

Long boots

Hacking jacket and tie for hunting or shows.

LESSON 27 | **Riding gear** continued

For cross country, riders are required
to wear a crash helmet and body protector,
under which a cotton jersey is usually worn.
A number bib is worn on top, and note the
medical card attached to the rider's arm—
this is now compulsory in many countries.

For advanced Dressage, top hat, tails, and spurs must be worn and whips cannot be carried. The number is attached to the horse's numnah.

For advanged show jumping, a coat in red, blue, green, or black is usually worn—the colors of the lapel and jacket usually denote the rider's country. Crash helmets must be worn.

LESSON 28 | **Safety gear**

Safety is the all-important factor when deciding on what equipment to acquire. Prioritize what you absolutely need and can afford—fashionable jodhpurs won't make you a better rider, but a safety helmet could save your life.

High-visibility clothing Minimum safety wear for riding on the road is a brightly colored jacket. At night, high-visibility clothing—originally used only by police forces—is now available to the general public in many forms.

Protective wear
A back protector is a padded waistcoat with extra protection for the shoulders and spine. It is an excellent safety precaution in case of a fall, and is often compulsory for competitive jumping.

Crash helmet
The head is the most vulnerable part of the body, and everyone should wear a safety helmet when riding. This should be light and conform to current safety standards, and the chin strap must be secured at all times when mounted.

Footwear
A heel is essential to prevent the foot slipping through the stirrup iron. Support around the ankle, and protection from lower leg chafing is also desirable.

Jodhpur boots are comfortable, practical, and safe; ankle boots can be teamed with chaps to protect the legs.

Long leather riding boots are expensive, but do give protection against chafing. A cheaper alternative is rubber riding boots.

LESSON 29 | **Western clothing**

Western clothes are designed for comfort and practicality.

It is essential to be correctly dressed for this type of riding. A wide-brimmed hat and long-sleeved shirt provide protection from the sun, and leather chaps worn on top of jeans prevent rubbing or soreness. Leather boots with high heels ensure the foot remains comfortably in the stirrups.

Although Western riding does not have strict rules on color and design of riding clothes for competition, as in European riding, there are still fashion considerations—in competition, your clothing will make the first impression, so make sure it is a good one. Get advice from a more experienced competitor, then choose clothing that suits you and expresses your personality.

Other essential clothes

- Blue denim has long been associated with cowboys—it is hard-wearing, comfortable, and easy to wash. The double stitching on the inner leg ensures the seam does not twist over and chafe the rider.

- Chaps wrap around the leg, protecting it from the saddle, and from ropes or branches across the thighs.

- Brightly colored and highly decorated cowboy boots—these should be comfortable as well as fashionable. Belts can be bought to match—the chaps are held up with these.

- Cowboy hats come in a range of shapes and colors—these are further customized by squashing and shaping the hat to fit.

- Bandanas are worn around the neck as decoration, and tied across the face to keep dust from the mouth and nose during cattle work.

Show time
This pair is rigged out for a show—the bridle and saddle are ornate, and the rider is wearing a peach shirt in delicate fabric, an ornate belt, and a blindingly white hat.

Everyday gear
This rider is wearing clothing suitable for work—simple, hard-wearing, and comfortable. His horse is also in a simple hard-wearing bridle, which will be easy to maintain and repair.

GROOMING ESSENTIALS

Grooming a horse has much more to it than merely improving the animal's appearance—it also helps to keep it healthy and feeling good. Here the essential grooming tools are covered, and also those that make life a little easier.

LESSON 30 | **Grooming kit**

Grooming is one of the most rewarding chores.

A glossy coat like this one can only be achieved by taking time and care over the grooming routine. It's also a good time to bond with your horse and look out for any problems

Not only does it help to clean the animal, but it also stimulates the circulation of the horse or pony. It is the perfect time to really get to know your horse, since a good grooming session will take up to three-quarters of an hour.

Grooming should be done on a daily basis with the stabled horse. Grass-kept horses and ponies should not be over-groomed however, because this will remove the natural oils that are keeping them warm. It should be enough just to pick out their feet and remove any mud and stains before tacking up. The basic grooming kit on page 88 is sufficient for everyday grooming—if you need to give your horse a bath, clip it, or prepare for a show, you will need extra kit, shown on page 89.

SEE ALSO
Basic grooming kit **page 188**
Winter care **page 154**
Summer care **page 155**
Clipping **page 148**
Competition grooming **page 158**

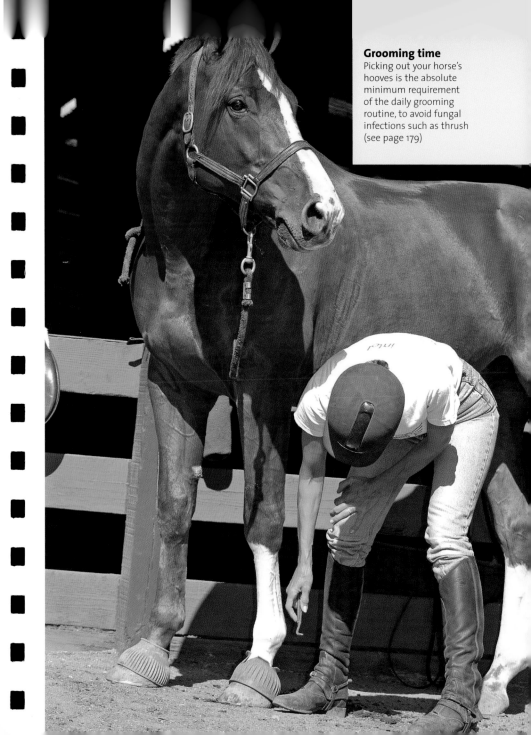

Grooming time
Picking out your horse's
hooves is the absolute
minimum requirement
of the daily grooming
routine, to avoid fungal
infections such as thrush
(see page 179)

LESSON 30 | **Grooming kit** continued

Basic grooming kit

▼ Stable rubber used all over the horse to give a final shine.

▼ Body brush used for removing grease and dust, and for cleaning the head and legs.

▲ Water brush used wet to lay the mane and tail, to bath the horse, or wash the feet.

▲ Rubber curry comb designed for all-over use on the horse. Applied in a circular motion, it brings grease to the surface.

▲ Plastic curry comb used for removing mud and tidying mane and tail. Children can use it for cleaning the body brush.

▲ Metal curry comb used for removing dirt from the body brush only and never on the horse.

◄ Metal combs for removing minor tangles and for "pulling" the mane and tail.

▶ Hoof pick used to pick out dirt from hooves.

▲ Sponge cut in two; one is used for wiping the face, and one under the dock. Replace these regularly.

▶ Dandy brush, a stiff brush for cleaning off mud or dirt from unclipped horses.

A basic grooming kit, which should be kept clean and washed approximately once a week.

Extended grooming kit

▼ Grooming mitt to remove grease, sweat, and mud from the coat—this has cactus cloth on one side, and sheepskin for polishing on the other.

▲ Round-ended scissors used to tidy the horse's heels, in conjunction with a mane comb, or to trim a small area of mane behind the ears as a "bridleway" for the bridle to rest comfortably.

▲ Cotton wool for wiping eyes and nostrils.

▲ Battery-powered trimmer for small areas, such as the face.

▲ Grooming brush that attaches to a household vacuum cleaner—you can also buy dedicated grooming machines, which loosen dust and grease and are best used on the horse once or twice a week with manual grooming in-between.

▲ Rubber grooming mitt to remove dirt; rub all over in a circular fashion.

▲ Hoof oil prevents the hooves from becoming dry and brittle in hot weather, and is used to give an attractive shine for competition.

▲ Sweat scraper for removing excess water after washing, or sweat after very hard work.

▲ Hairbrush—preferred by some people for brushing out tails without damaging hairs.

Most grooming kit can be bought in various colors and designs; if you have more than one horse, you can buy kit for each horse in different colors to prevent cross contamination.

◄ Electric clippers (see page 148).

Free time
Horses love to gallop and roll when loose—
they will either get very dusty or very
muddy—owners of gray horses are at a
definite disadvantage because of the extra
grooming required!

RIDING BASICS

The two basic riding styles practiced today are Western and European.

The history of Western riding can be traced as far back as the sixteenth century. Today, the working cattle horse remains an essential part of many American ranches, but it is in the show ring that Western riding has become popular worldwide. Any horse can be trained in the Western manner, and you don't necessarily need to use the special tack (although the Western equipment does undoubtedly lend a certain authenticity).

European riding in its highest form is displayed at the Olympics. Riding in this style takes place worldwide; the American equestrian team is highly respected alongside the traditional European teams of Great Britain, France, and Germany.

Both styles of riding require the same skills, often applied in subtly different ways. In this chapter basic information about how to ride in each style is given, which is not an alternative to riding lessons, but may help you to improve faster, and make fewer initial mistakes. Remember, everyone falls off; the trick is to get back on and learn from the experience.

Western riding is becoming more popular worldwide, as are the Western breeds: the Paint horse (left) and the Quarter horse (right).

LESSON 31 | **European mounting and dismounting**

Mounting

For the beginner, the first important achievement is getting on and off the horse correctly. The aim is to mount and dismount in a fluid movement that does not pull at the horse's back or alarm the horse in any way.

Before mounting, always check the girth and pull down both stirrups. Choose a safe, flat area and ensure the reins are in place. Always mount from the near (left) side of the horse.

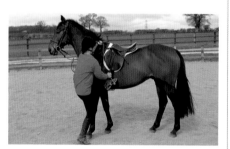

1 Hold the reins so the horse is under control. Face the quarters, hold the stirrup, and place the left foot into the iron.

2 With your right hand on the cantle, swivel toward the horse and push your weight down into the stirrup. Jump upward until you are standing with your weight in the left stirrup.

3 Swing your right leg over the quarters and ease yourself into the saddle. Place your right foot into the stirrup and sit centrally in the saddle.

The mounting block enables the rider to mount with relative comfort without twisting or stretching the saddle, or pulling the horse's back.

Dismounting

1 At halt, hold the reins in your left hand. Take both feet out of the stirrups and swing forward.

2 Swing your right leg over, making sure you clear the quarters—a kick will make the horse jump.

3 Land on both feet with flexed knees facing the horse. Take the reins over the horse's head and run up the stirrup irons on both sides.

LESSON 32 | **European control and aids**

The aids are the means by which the rider tells the horse what to do. They consist of the rider's hands, legs, and seat. All riding comes from a good seat—the rider must always be balanced, relaxed, and moving with the horse.

Head upright and looking in direction of travel.

Hands just above the withers with fingers loosely rounded inward and thumbs uppermost.

Shoulders relaxed but upright and back straight, but not stiff.

Elbows bent and arms relaxed and close to sides.

Upper legs flat against the saddle with relaxed hips, knees, and ankles. Lower legs against the horse's sides.

Balls of the feet should rest lightly in the stirrups, with the weight in the heels.

The seat
The shoulder, hip, and heel should remain on a perpendicular line, with the weight evenly distributed.

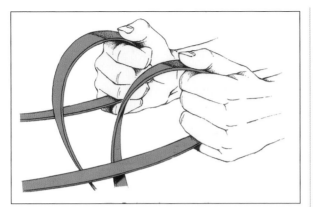

The hands

The reins pass between the fourth and little fingers, then through the palms and between thumb and first finger. The contact should be light and relaxed. The hands should remain passive—pulling the horse's head about results in a fed-up horse with a hard mouth, and often no change in direction.

The legs

Nudges or little vibratory kicks should be used—constant kicking results in "dead-sides" or over-responsive bolting. The legs are applied just behind the girth and must hang loosely. (For use of legs to create changes in speed see page 98.)

Turning left

Squeeze the left rein and keep the left leg on the girth. The right rein should lie along the neck—the horse will move away from this pressure. Your right leg should apply pressure just behind the girth, so that the horse is encouraged to curve, not swivel. To turn right, reverse the instructions.

Moving diagonally (half pass)

The left leg is slightly behind the girth and the left seat bone presses down, pushing the horse to the right. The right leg keeps the horse moving forward. Both hands are neutral, so the horse faces ahead.

Moving backward (reining back)

In halt, squeeze both reins to prevent forward movement, and use both legs just behind the girth. To halt, relax both hands and the legs.

Stopping (halt)

Legs relax, but hold the horse straight if necessary. Squeeze both reins, and press down with both seat bones. Reins should be relaxed when the horse halts.

LESSON 33 | **European—riding the paces**

Proper schooling results in a horse that moves smoothly from one gait to the next. The aids for moving up one pace are outlined below. In order to slow down, shift your weight backward and squeeze the reins.

Walk
At the halt, release pressure on the reins, and squeeze gently with both legs. Sit square, allowing your body and hands to move with the horse's head. To push on, squeeze gently with alternate legs as the horse sways.

Trot
At the walk, squeeze gently with both legs. Sit for two or three trotting strides then rise as the horse's inner shoulder comes forward. Sit as it goes back, then rise. This is rising trot. You will also need to master sitting trot—sitting in the saddle and moving with the horse.

SEE ALSO
The paces **page 22**

Canter

A good canter is easier when the horse is on a corner. At sitting trot, squeeze gently with the outer leg behind the girth and the inner leg on the girth. This causes the horse to "lead" with its inner foreleg, and be balanced. Sit deep in the saddle, and move with the motion of the horse.

The counter canter is a circle purposefully cantered on the wrong leg—it requires great balance from horse and rider.

A flying change is achieved by reversing the aids—the horse will swap leading legs, which allows it to corner in the opposite direction without losing balance. This is very useful in show jumping.

Gallop At the canter, lean forward with your weight slightly out of the saddle and squeeze gently. You must maintain an even contact with short reins since pulling or shifting of weight could seriously unbalance the horse. Horses enjoy galloping, but you must ensure the surface is suitable and the horse is under control.

LESSON 34 | **Western mounting and dismounting**

Remember, when mounting and dismounting, it is always important to pick a safe spot and have the horse under control.

Mounting is done the same way as European style (see page 94), except that you must remember that the Western saddle is higher, so you will need to swing your leg up that little bit farther before settling into the saddle. The position in the saddle is practically the same except that a slightly longer leg is adopted. However, it is essential to have some degree of flexion in the knee and ankle to ensure adequate balance, and enable you to rise up out of the saddle when mounting and dismounting. The hands are positioned above the horn and the reins may be held Texan or Californian style (see page 102).

Dismounting is done in much the same way as European style (see page 95) but taking one leg at a time.

Mounting

1 Stand on the near side facing forward and take hold of the reins with your left hand and the horn with your right.

Dismounting

1 Holding the reins in your left hand, and with your right hand on the horn, take your right foot out of the stirrup.

2 Push down in the stirrup with your left foot and pull yourself forward and up with the horn. Swing your right leg up over the saddle.

3 Once you have settled into the saddle, place the right foot into the stirrup and take up the reins.

2 Lean forward slightly from the hips and swing the right leg back and over the quarters. Step down with your right foot.

3 Take your left foot out of the stirrup and release your hold on the horn. Some Western horses ground tie (stand still when the reins are dropped on the floor) but this is not advisable for long periods.

LESSON 35 | **Western control and aids**

As with all riding, sitting straight in the saddle and evenly distributing your weight down into the heel play important parts. The leg should hang comfortably down but still must enable you to rise up out of the saddle.

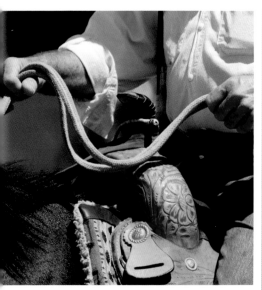

The Californian method (closed)
Both reins come up through the palm of one hand and out between the thumb and first finger. The romal (end) goes through the spare hand and is used as a whip.

The Texan method (open)
The reins are held between the thumb and first finger of one hand and pass down through the palm. The reins are not joined and hang loosely across the thigh.

Neck reining (turning)

The horse moves away from the rein on its neck and the leg on its side. All Western riding uses subtle commands—the rider must cease the aid when the horse responds.

To turn left, the reins must be moved over to the left-hand side, so that they rest on the right side of the neck. Stay straight in the saddle with the right leg on the girth and the left leg behind the girth.

Straightness in the saddle is essential for good Western riding. If riding one-handed, the reins are held in the left hand and the right hand should remain on the right thigh, or on the horn. Keep your rein hand comfortably just above or in front of the horn, but never so high that it causes you to lean forward.

Neck reining in action
Even at high speed, this horse turns sharply when asked.

LESSON 36 | **Western—riding the paces**

Western riding has different paces, and a different rhythm to European riding, but the more relaxed style of riding requires just as much skill.

Walk This horse is stretching down and relaxing after a work session. Note the rider's balanced position with a straight line between her shoulders from the hips to the heels. The horse should at all times be pushed on from the seat, and the reins should be loose—the weight of the reins is enough to keep contact with a well-trained horse. Practice halting, turning, and reining back smoothly—the horse will also need to cope with obstacles and opening gates for Western shows. Putting on a coat while the horse remains still requires obedience and trust.

SEE ALSO
The paces **page 22**

Jog A slower, smoother pace than the European trot, the horse must remain in a consistent rhythm and be smooth, with easy, accurate transitions. The rider does not rise to the trot, and the gait should be comfortable enough to continue for hours.

Lope The lope or canter is a slow pace, very smooth and controlled, and extremely comfortable. The horse needs to be beautifully balanced to perform this correctly and the rider must be supple in the hips to be able to move easily in time to the animal's movements. This rider is bareback, and perfectly balanced.

Advanced work Advanced training includes flying lead changes, spins, sliding stops, and rollbacks (turns on the haunches). Most of these are fast but smooth versions of Dressage movements, mostly indicated by the rider's seat rather than hand or leg aids. The spin is particularly spectacular to watch, with the horse making a series of 360-degree turns.

The sliding stop is purely a show movement. It requires special shoes to achieve the right effect and protective boots to prevent injury to the forelegs. The horse learns to halt from a gallop, tucking its hind legs well underneath it, with its back rounded and neck arched, as it slides anything up to nearly 30 feet (9 m) to a stop.

The rein back requires great trust on the part of the horse, because it cannot see immediately behind. The horse must respond to the lightest touch on the reins.

LESSON 37 | **Horse handling**

Handling your horse is an exercise in common sense—always do things sensibly, quietly, and safely. Never forget that your horse has a mind of its own, and is bigger and heavier than you.

Leading with a halter
Keep one hand under the chin, and hold the slack rope in your other hand. Never put your finger through the ring of the halter or in a loop of rope.

SEE ALSO
Body language **page 24**
Behavioural science **page 28**
Common vices **page 30**

Leading with a bridle

Take the reins over your horse's head, and hold in the same way as a halter. Always walk on the near (left) side of the horse.

Feeding a treat

Hold treats on your palm with fingers together. Horses can't see under their noses, and may mistake fingers for carrots.

Riding on the road

Ridden horses are considered to be vehicles and must go in the same direction as traffic, as close to the side of the road as possible. When leading horses, keep between them and the traffic. These rules are more or less the same worldwide, but always check local rules when riding.

Catching your horse

Some horses are difficult to catch unless you take food with you. Hold out the food, and slip the rope around the horse's neck. Put the halter over its head and do it up. As you lead the horse, keep the bucket in your spare hand.

LESSON 38| **Schooling**

Basic schooling is the physical and mental education of the horse. Like an athlete, a horse needs to be fit if it is going to perform to its best ability.

A horse has to be prepared in a logical way to bring it up to a fit condition, one where it is happy to be ridden, responds to signals from the rider, and is obedient and co-operative. A horse should be schooled gradually, starting at an elementary level. Some schooling exercises are discussed on these two pages.

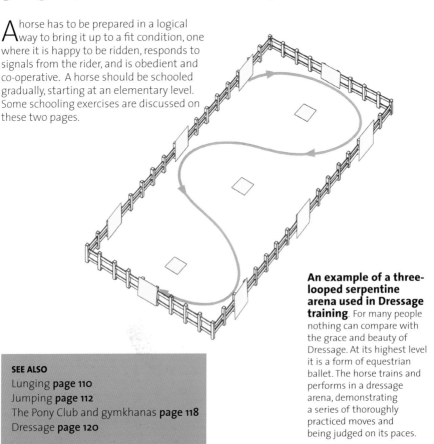

An example of a three-looped serpentine arena used in Dressage training. For many people nothing can compare with the grace and beauty of Dressage. At its highest level it is a form of equestrian ballet. The horse trains and performs in a dressage arena, demonstrating a series of thoroughly practiced moves and being judged on its paces.

SEE ALSO
Lunging **page 110**
Jumping **page 112**
The Pony Club and gymkhanas **page 118**
Dressage **page 120**

Jumping ideas

- Ride over grids of poles and fences to loosen and strengthen the horse.

- A pole 9–10 feet (2.75–3.1 m) before single fences slows "rushing" horses.

- A pole behind the fence will have the same effect and encourage it to arch over the fence.

- Practice doubles and triple combinations so that the horse is confident at seeing two or three fences in a line.

- Build small courses of three or four jumps and ride smoothly from fence to fence.

- Jump logs and tires and walk through water to prepare for cross country.

Flat work

- Ride bareback and concentrate on balance.

- Ride without reins to improve your leg aids.

- Work evenly on both reins to prevent one side being overworked.

- Mark out a school and ride circles and serpentines (see opposite).

- Work on changing paces smoothly and on collecting and extending.

- Develop the canter for jumping so that you can shorten and lengthen the stride without losing balance, rhythm, or impulsion.

Keep schooling varied

Try different things when you ride, since your horse will get bored with repetition. Alternate flat work, jumping, and riding out in the countryside—remember that you should be training your horse constantly. Wherever you are, your horse should always be under control.

LESSON 39 | **Lunging**

Lunge work involves the horse moving around the trainer on an outside circle attached to a lunge line.

The trainer stays in the center and encourages the horse forward with a lunge whip. A triangle is formed between the trainer, the horse, and the whip.

Lunging is a controlled way of exercising a horse without riding it—the ring in which the exercise takes place should be as large as possible and have a good ground surface. A tight circle puts additional strain on the limbs, but a carefully monitored lunging program can help build up a horse's strength and increase suppleness.

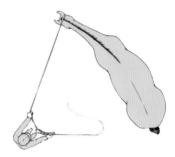

Lunging technique
Positioned behind the point of the shoulder, the trainer gradually increases the size of the circle, controlling the head with the left hand and the hindquarters with the whip in the right. The aim is to get the horse to walk, trot, and halt correctly, responding to verbal commands.

Lunging in a circle
The horse is wearing full lunge kit, and is trotting in a large circle. To increase the diameter, the trainer can walk sideways in a circle.

Lunging over jumps

A well-trained horse can be lunged over large jumps to increase confidence and give experience without the added weight of a rider.

Raised poles on a slight circle will increase balance and concentration.

Lunging or long reining is also used by Western trainers and whisperers (see page 26); however, it is usually less formal and concentrates on body language of horse and trainer.

LESSON 40 | **Jumping**

The horse is a natural jumper—in the wild it can be seen leaping over bushes, ditches, and puddles. When ridden, it must adjust its balance to compensate for the rider.

Jumping technique

The rider is looking toward the next jump, pushing the horse on into her hands so that its legs come well underneath its body, and its nose lowers to allow it to see and judge the height of the jump.

SEE ALSO

The paces **page 22**
Show jumping **page 122**
Eventing **page 124**

Poles are a useful start—place three or four approximately 3 yards (3 m) apart for horses. Swing slightly forward as the horse lifts off and then sit up as it lands. Practice your approach absolutely straight, then later approach from a turn or a large circle, aiming for a steady canter.

Cross poles encourage the horse to aim for the center of the fence. Ride a straight approach and ride away straight afterward to prepare for jumping another.

A series of poles and fences in a grid is an excellent training exercise. Build up gradually, and concentrate on maintaining impulsion. Sit up over poles and go with the horse over the fences. This is excellent training for jumping doubles and trebles.

To clear the fence, the horse brings its legs fully underneath to spring off them from a good canter. The rider keeps her weight forward over the withers, and allows the horse its head, while maintaining contact.

On the track
Racehorses often wear specialist bridle attachments—the large noseband means the horse lowers its head and concentrates; the blinkers prevent the horse from being distracted.

COMPETITIVE RIDING

This chapter is an introduction to the wide variety of equestrian sports that can be enjoyed. The section includes Dressage, show jumping, eventing, racing, Western show, and rodeo. Each unit gives an indication of what is involved and how to succeed. Other sports such as polo, vaulting, and Pony Club and gymkhana games are also covered.

To compete at the top requires years of dedication (and often frustration), but nothing can surpass the atmosphere of major competitions. Nothing is more exciting than the roar of the crowd, the commentator's announcements, and the sensation of entering the ring to perform, after months of hard work and training.

Barrel racing (left) is a fast and exhilarating rodeo event. Although some men compete at amateur level, professionally it is an event for women.

LESSON 41 | **The Pony Club and gymkhanas**

Pony clubs are popular across the world, and the organization was started to produce responsible riders who rode well and cared for their ponies properly. Today, there are over 100,000 club members in 20 countries.

For many children, the most important aspect of Pony Club membership lies in the gymkhana games—events played as team sports in competitions only open to members. Local shows also run classes and gymkhana games with open entry. The Secretary of the Show handles the entries into each event or class— it is your responsibility to ensure you meet the criteria for entry.

Showing is split into breed and type classes; pictured is a stunning Arab being shown in-hand. The judge chooses the horse that most conforms to breed type. Classes are either ridden or in-hand, and at higher levels the horse and handler must have showmanship as well as a beautiful turn-out.

Dressage classes require you to learn the Dressage test beforehand—it will be available from the Secretary. Young riders can also enter riding classes, which are a good springboard into Dressage.

Gymkhana games are divided into different age groups, and offer something for everyone. Leading-rein games enable very young children the chance to compete. Practice is essential, as is good control and balance.

Show jumping allows children to compete on a lead rein or there are three levels: novice, intermediate, and advanced. Classes are further split by height of horse—novice 10–12-hand ponies will be asked to jump something far smaller than novice over 15-hand horses.

LESSON 42 | **Dressage**

A well turned-out novice pair halt before beginning the test. Horses must demonstrate simple movements obediently in a snaffle bridle with simple noseband. Riders should wear tweed, navy, or black jackets with white breeches and black hunting boots.

Dressage is the word used to describe training the ridden horse on the flat. Equestrian ballet can only be performed at the highest level after years of practice by both horse and rider.

Every rider performs a set routine of movements and paces. The judges look for quality of paces as well as correct execution of the movements. Circles must be perfect, and the horse must go willingly; signs of tension lose marks. The judges write comments on test sheets, which give guidance to the rider after the test.

SEE ALSO
Saddle extras **page 54**
Nosebands, bits, and bridles
   page 56
Riding gear **page 78**
European control and aids **page 78**
Competition grooming **page 158**

The passage, an elevated trot, in an advanced-level competition. At high levels a double bridle and Dressage saddle must be used. The rider should wear a tailcoat and top hat.

Half pass is very advanced; the horse travels diagonally, curved in the direction of travel. Horses wear support bandages in training, but they are not allowed in competition.

Extended trot (left) and collected trot (above)

Collection and extension become more intense as the horse progresses up the grades.

LESSON 43 | **Show jumping**

Essentially, show jumping consists of riding over a series of unfixed obstacles in a set course.

U sually, the winner is the rider with the fewest faults (penalties) or in case of a tie, the fastest time. Fences come in all shapes and sizes, but fall into basic types:

Verticals, such as the wall and gate, have no spread.
Spreads consist of width as well as height (see right).
Combinations consist of two or three fences with one or two strides between each.

The Federation Equestrian Internationale sets international jumping penalties; check local rules before competing. Usually four faults are given if the horse refuses a fence or knocks it down. Refusal inside combinations means rejumping the combination. Two refusals or a fall result in elimination. Time faults are given if you go over the course time limit.

After all the competitors have jumped the course, either the prize goes to the rider with the fewest points, or, if there is more than one rider with a clear round, it goes to a jump off. Each rider goes again over a shorter course—a great deal of strategy is involved, since now the winner will be the possessor of the fastest clear round. A well-balanced horse that turns quickly is a great asset in jump offs.

Before competing, familiarize yourself with the obstacles and distances by walking the course on foot. Check where the start and finish are and plan your turns, walking the distances between fences. Ride in the ring as you would at home, in a well-balanced canter. If something goes wrong, stay calm and keep going; the experience will improve both you and your horse. Never take out your disappointment on your horse.

The rider looks at the next fence while airborne—this saves time and gets the horse balanced and moving in the right direction directly after landing.

LESSON 44 | **Eventing**

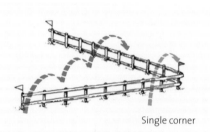

Single corner

Double combination

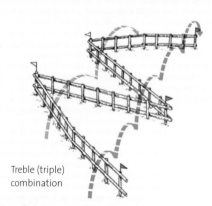

Treble (triple)
combination

Cross-country combinations

Here you can see three combinations
with slower and easier (red) and quicker
and more difficult (blue) routes marked.

Eventing is a challenge for the rider, and requires a special horse.

The partnership must perform
three disciplines to a high standard,
demanding fitness, stamina, agility,
and obedience.

Three-day eventing is the top level of
competition. Dressage is performed on the
first day, cross country on the second, and
show jumping on the third. Faults from
show jumping and cross country are added
to the Dressage score to give a final total.
The horse and rider with the lowest score
is the winner.

Riding cross country

Many fences and combinations in cross
country are designed to give riders choices—
usually there will be a faster, tricky option
and a slower, easier option. It is up to the
rider to choose the best course for their
horse, and for the conditions.

SEE ALSO
Dressage **page 120**
Show jumping **page 122**
Fitness for competition **page 162**
Vet checks **page 167**

Water jumps have a small obstacle into a lake, then one or two strides through water before a second jump.

Drop jumps have a landing much lower than the take off—or higher. The horse will not know until airborne, so the rider must be in control.

Cross-country fences are solid—making a mistake will not knock down fences, but horses can scramble over jumps with a tabletop like this one.

LESSON 45 | **Polo and vaulting**

Vaulting

Gymnastics and riding come together in this unusual equestrian pastime. Riders learn such things as the art of somersaulting away and landing. For voltige, the horse must be calm and tough, with a smooth, even canter, and ideally have a fairly flat, broad back.

The vaulting roller is a specially adapted roller with padding, hand grips, and foot loops. This Belgian Draught horse has an ideal temperament for vaulting.

Children often enjoy vaulting, and have naturally good balance. Comfortable clothes and shoes with flexible soft soles are a necessity—hard hats are useful for beginners. The horse will need boots or bandages, and a lunging bridle.

The **"ponies,"** usually 15–15.2 hands must be quick and agile to stop, turn, and accelerate when required. Tough, wiry, fast, and very strong, these amazing animals are highly intelligent. Many learn to watch the ball and help the players with their quick-wittedness.

Polo

The fast and furious game of polo is the oldest and fastest stick-and-ball game, and is the national pastime in Argentina. Boys learn the game at an early age, and the greatest polo ponies in the world are bred there and sold to the top players around the world.

The game has a handicapping system; players are rated according to performance. By matching team totals or by crediting lesser-rated teams with a goal advantage, even matches are made up.

Players use bamboo cane mallets played in the right hand. They wear white breeches, long brown boots, helmets, and a team jersey. The horses have heavily bandaged legs for support when turning and stopping quickly.

LESSON 46 | **Racing**

It takes breeding, training, and a lot of luck to produce a champion for the "sport of kings."

This worldwide spectator sport supports a massive gambling industry, and fortunes have been lost and won on the nose of a galloping racehorse.

Flat races

Flat races are started with an electric starting gate. The tactics and riding ability of the jockeys, in conjunction with the trainer's instructions, often determine the success or failure of the horse. However, a good horse is always striving to be at the front.

Grass tracks are the norm in Europe, but in the United States most races are run on a specially formulated dirt track. This consists of a firm base with approximately 4 inches (10 cm) of dirt on top. Some horses run better on a particular surface, and may be shipped abroad to compete on whatever is most suitable.

Horses starting from the gate on a grass track.

Hurdles are smaller than fences, and give way when hit, so most racehorses begin their career over hurdles

Steeplechasing

Steeplechasing came about in Britain in the eighteenth century; the first recorded race took place in Ireland in 1752, over a distance of 4.5 miles (7 km), using church steeples as the most obvious landmarks in the countryside (hence the name steeplechase). By the turn of the twentieth century, steeplechasing had become an established sport, with races taking place worldwide.

It is usual for steeplechasers to start their careers in hurdle races before progressing to bigger fences. In the United States, equine steeplechasers race younger than those in Britain, often starting out as three- or four-year-olds, although five or six is more usual for steeplechasing. Races take place over 2–4 miles (3–6 km), and are rarely started from electric starting gates.

SEE ALSO
Thoroughbred breed **page 13**

LESSON 47 | **Western show classes**

A Saddlebred Western pleasure horse and rider ready for competition.

SEE ALSO
Western clothing **page 84**
The Pony Club and gymkhanas **page 118**
Dressage **page 120**

There are numerous show classes, all derived from the practical use of the working horse.

The American Quarter Horse Association has its own shows and classes, but various specialist associations and breed societies have Western riding classes worldwide with their own variation on these.

Western pleasure classes are ideal for beginners. The horse must be a pleasure to ride at the walk, jog, and lope (canter), on a fairly loose rein, and it should demonstrate its obedience and smoothness of action.

Trail classes require the horse to deal with three mandatory obstacles: a gate to open and close, four logs to be ridden over, and an obstacle to be backed through or around. Other tests may include water, stepping through obstacles, and mailing letters. The horse's paces and fluency are taken into account.

Western riding tests the all-round training of the ranch horse, proving it to be versatile, well mannered, and comfortable while performing various obstacles and a set "pattern" (course). This starts in the walk and finishes with a rein back.

Working cow horse is designed to show the versatility of the general ranch horse, and is divided into two sections—reining and cattle working. The scores are added together to determine the overall winner.

Reining is high-adrenaline Dressage at speed, performed in a fluid and smooth manner with near-invisible aids from the rider. Patterns include lead changes, transitions, spins, rollbacks, sliding stops, and slow and fast circles.

A young cowboy prepares for in-hand showing with an attractive Palomino. In the United States, the Palomino is classed as a breed, not just a coat color.

High-adrenaline riding in the reining competition—contrast this with the extended canter of a Dressage competition.

The slide stop—the horse skids a good distance almost on his hocks, and needs support bandages and special shoes.

Turning at full speed requires balance from both horse and rider.

LESSON 48 | **Rodeo riding**

Based on techniques perfected by Mexican vaqueros, American rodeos were originally organized by cowboys to entertain themselves and their families in their spare time. Nowadays, rodeo is a sport with huge pay checks for successful professionals.

Cutting has some of the highest prize money of any equestrian sport. The cutting horse has an instinct for separating particular identified calves from the herd. The rider must sit and stay with the horse's movement without interfering once they have indicated to the horse which calf to take. Many have the chance to cut out another calf in the two-and-a-half minutes.

SEE ALSO
American Quarter horse breed **page 10**
Western show classes **page 130**

Saddle bronco riding is based on the rough and tough methods used by early cowboys to "break" wild horses, and is considered one of the most demanding events. The cowboy must try to remain on a bucking horse for eight seconds, with only a basic saddle and halter for security.

Bareback riding is perhaps the most dangerous of the riding contests, because there is only a hand-hold for support and the horse's head is left free. Tremendous balance and strength in the riding arm is required to remain on board.

Steer wrestling is performed with two cowboys, two horses and a steer, and the contestant. The cowboys chase the steer on horseback, then one dismounts onto the steer and deftly brings it down.

In the wild horse race, each team of three must saddle their wild horse, then ride over the finishing line—with ten horses in the ring, it is chaotic!

Barrel racing involves racing around three barrels in a clover-leaf formation. Speed and agility are particularly important, and American Quarter horses are usually outstanding in this event.

HORSE CARE

Your horse relies on you to take care of its everyday needs. Whether a top eventer or a family pet, it deserves the best you can give to ensure health and well being. Food, shelter, and exercise are vital to all horses—while geographical locations will inevitably dictate different ways of doing certain things, the basics remain the same worldwide.

This section is split into two—first, general horse care is discussed, with practical how-to guides on caring for your horse in all seasons. In the second section we look more closely at how to care for a competition horse—differences in feeding, fitness, and readiness for competition.

The joys of the horse
Horses are beautiful animals that deserve the best you can provide. In return, you will get companionship and loyalty.

HORSE CARE ESSENTIALS

In this section, the essentials of horse care are covered: grooming, feeding, shoeing, teeth, fitness, and mucking out.

LESSON 49 | **Mucking out**

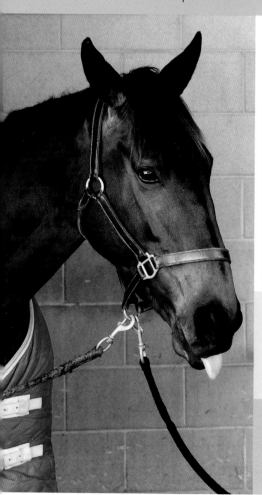

Cleanliness is an absolute essential in the stall or stable.

This section is for owners of horses kept in a stable, all or part of the time.

Mucking out your horse should be done every day; if the horse is in the stable all day, it will need to be done morning and evening. For safety reasons, tie up your horse securely before mucking out, or use a rope across the door to keep the horse in while you get in and out easily.

Two-rope tether
Tethering with two ropes prevents an edgy horse from turning around or kicking.

SEE ALSO
Stabling **page 40**
Bedding **page 44**

Mucking out method

1 Use a four-tined fork to pick up droppings, and a shovel to remove any damp patches of sawdust or peat. Put the droppings in a large bucket, then use a wheelbarrow to transfer it to the muck heap.
2 Fluff up straw bedding with the fork, and bank bedding around the edges of the stable so if the horse rolls it is less likely to get cast (stuck).
3 Check the horse has a clean water source and a full hay net.
4 Regularly clean out the whole stable: hose and scrub the floor and allow it to dry before remaking the bed; this will help discourage rats and insects, and prevent build up of bacteria and fungi in the bedding.

Securing your horse

When tying up your horse, always use a quick-release knot. Horses can panic when tied, fall, and injure themselves badly. To avoid this, tie your lead rope to a loop of string, which will break if the horse struggles.

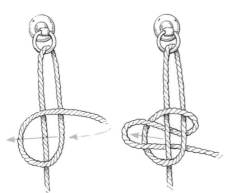

The rope end can be tucked through the loop, but must be pulled out to undo the knot.

LESSON 50 | **Basic grooming**

Grooming is one of the most satisfying moments of horse care and gives you the best chance of getting to know your horse and all its little eccentricities.

Golden rules

- Always tie up your horse before grooming.

- Never groom a damp horse.

- Never stand in front of or behind your horse.

- Always pick out hooves before and after riding, or at least once a day.

- Always groom the saddle and girth area before tacking up.

- Work from the front to the back of your horse.

- Follow the same routine each time.

- Keep your kit clean.

- Make sure you and your horse enjoy it.

SEE ALSO

Basic grooming kit **page 88**
Mucking out **page 138**
Winter care **page 154**
Summer care **page 155**

Grooming is the perfect opportunity to check for any illness or injury; and to prevent it—carefully cleaning the hooves and saddle area before tacking up and riding helps to stop saddle sores and lameness. On these two pages is a good basic grooming routine, but for competitions (see pages 158–161) a different routine will be necessary. As an absolute minimum, pick out the hooves and brush the saddle and girth area before riding.

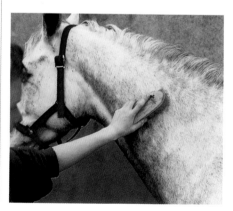

Dandy brushing Beginning at the top of the neck with the dandy brush, groom rhythmically downward in a semicircular motion toward the tail. Knock out the hairs from the brush against a wall every few strokes. Do not use the dandy brush on clipped areas.

Body brushing Repeat the first step with the body brush. After every two strokes scrape the brush through the curry comb. Never use the curry comb on the horse. Use the body brush to clean the horse's face and legs—be gentle.

Finger brushing Run your fingers through the horse's tail to remove tangles ("fingering"). Don't stand directly behind the horse. Once a week brush out the tail with the body brush; if you do this too often your horse's tail may get a bit thin!

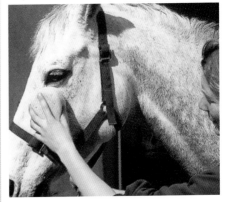

Curry combing If your horse has a short mane, you can keep it tidy with a plastic curry comb or the body brush (see above). A long mane will require fingering and a mane comb. Brush the forelock smooth on the face using the body brush.

Sponging Use a sponge to clean around the horse's eyes and nostrils. Use a second sponge to clean the dock area under the tail. Always keep the sponges separate and clean them after every use.

LESSON 51 | **Feeds and feeding**

Correct feeding requires the advice of an experienced professional. However, there are certain rules of feeding that will help to minimize any problems.

Horse size should determine feed amount—small ponies can be very greedy though!

SEE ALSO
Pasture **page 46**
Safety and security **page 48**

Overfeeding your horse or pony causes it to get fat, over-fresh, and suffer from health problems. Size determines amount of feed, but temperament, condition, and workload are also important.

Feed little and often since horses have small stomachs. In the wild, they spend around 18 hours a day grazing, so food "trickles" through the stomach; if it is overloaded, food is not digested properly, causing health problems.

Turn your horse out daily if you can. Grass contains roughage (fiber stimulates the gut to work efficiently) and 70–80 percent water. If the horse cannot eat grass it should be fed hay for fiber and succulents for moisture.

Horses are creatures of habit, so feed at the same time every day. Feed all the horses in a stable block at the same time. For groups of horses in fields, put food down in small piles—horses can become aggressive at mealtimes.

After feeding allow at least an hour before you exercise. A full stomach squashes the lungs, interfering with breathing. Undigested food is pushed into the intestines causing colic.

Never change your horse's food suddenly because bacteria and enzymes in the gut need time to adapt. Introduce new food along with the existing feed for at least a week.

A hay net is a good alternative to a hay rack. Tie it up with a safety knot (see page 139) and ensure it is at the horse's head height.

Always ensure that fresh water is available. If the horse drinks from streams, check that the area is safe and the water clean and easy to get to.

LESSON 51 | **Feeds and feeding** continued

Fiber feeds

Grass is the most natural feed and should be the main food where possible.

Hay is dried mature grass and has less nutritional value than young grass. It must be stored carefully because it can spontaneously combust.

Haylage is vacuum-packed still damp grass; it retains most of its nutritional value and is dust-free. It must be fed within four days of being opened.

Chop or chaff is a mixture of hay, barley, or oat straw, and/or alfalfa, chopped into short lengths. It often has added herbs, molasses, vitamins, and minerals.

Straw is a good source of fiber for ponies with laminitis (see page 182). Oat or barley is best since wheat straw is indigestible.

Alfalfa is a high protein and fiber feed. It is good for respiratory problems and laminitic ponies.

Grain feeds

Oats are high in fiber but low in energy and calcium. Oats can be fed whole or bruised. Naked oats are higher in energy and oil.

Barley is higher in energy but lower in fiber than oats. It has a hard outer coat, so cannot be fed whole without either soaking or boiling in water for an hour.

Bran is the outer coat of the wheat husk, and is high in phosphorus and fiber. A bran mash is made by pouring in boiling water and leaving it to soak for half an hour.

Corn or maize is higher in energy than barley and oats but low in protein. It is good for shy eaters because of the ration of energy gained to amount fed.

Supplements

Sugar beet is a good source of calcium and fiber. Before use it must be soaked for 12 hours or it doubles in size in the stomach, causing colic (see page 183).

Oil is a very effective slow-release source of energy with no starch or protein. Most pellets contain oils, but you can add 4 tablespoons (60 ml) of vegetable oil a day to other feeds to increase energy and add shine to the coat.

Carrots, apples, and root vegetables should be given whenever possible to add interest. Carrots should be cut lengthwise, because round pieces can cause choking.

Mineral feed blocks are very popular and give vital mineral and vitamin supplements.

LESSON 52 | **Shoeing**

There's a lot of truth in the old saying, "No foot, no horse." Healthy feet are essential to a horse's well being.

Hooves have to be trimmed at the right angle to keep them balanced and in good condition, and shod correctly for the type of work expected of the horse. There are many different types of shoe, and it is best to discuss your horse's requirements with your farrier. Horses are shod with iron or steel metal shoes, either fullered (grooved) or plain. Fullered shoes are lighter and give better grip.

Even ponies and horses that do not need to wear shoes need their hooves trimmed and shaped every four to eight weeks. Ponies that do not go on the road, or have hard hooves, may not need to wear shoes—check with a farrier.

Ask the farrier to pick up your foal's hooves and tap them when he checks the mare's hooves—this will make the foal easier to shoe in later life.

SEE ALSO
Points of the horse **page 14**
Winter care **page 154**
Summer care **page 155**
Lameness **page 181**

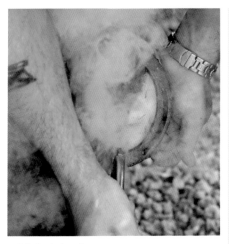

With hot shoeing, it is possible for the farrier to change the shape of the shoe to properly fit the foot. Here the farrier holds the hot shoe on the hoof—it does not hurt, but smoothes the hoof to fit better.

With cold shoeing, the shoe is pre-cast in different sizes designed to fit most feet. Nails are hammered into the hoof wall—it doesn't hurt, just like it doesn't hurt when you trim your nails.

Four different shoes Top left: aluminum racing plate. Bottom left: wide web shoe with larger weight-bearing surface. Top right: general-purpose front shoe. Bottom right: general-purpose hind shoe.

For competitive work, it is a good idea to use studs for extra grip—these are like football studs, and help the horse not to slip at speed. You can screw these in yourself with a spanner into pre-drilled holes in the heel of the shoe.

LESSON 53 | **Clipping**

Clipping is necessary only when horses undertake regular hard work, especially in winter when a thick coat increases sweating during heavy exercise. Usually, only part of the body is clipped to reduce sweating and keep the horse clean and cool.

How to clip your horse

Choose a safe area with good light.

- Thoroughly groom the horse.
- Use a blanket to prevent chills.
- Start at the front and work in sections.
- Repeat until smooth.
- Clip against the lie of the coat.
- Keep the blades flat on the skin.
- Keep blades well oiled to avoid overheating.
- Lift the front legs to clip the chest.
- Brush the horse all over when finished.
- Blanket the horse immediately.

SEE ALSO
Winter care **page 154**
Summer care **page 155**

The head and face are the most difficult parts to clip. Make sure the horse is kept calm and its head is held still while clipping this area. Trimming whiskers may prove a ticklish job. The careful use of scissors or a razor may be an alternative.

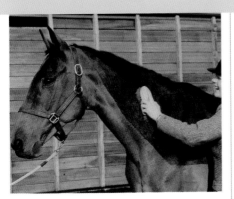

Trace clipping removes a line of hair along the neck, under the belly, and from the upper part of the legs. It is suitable for horses doing less strenuous exercise, or for those who are to be kept at grass.

The hunter clip is for hard work in muddy situations. The long hair on their legs protects from mud and hedge scratches when going cross country. The saddle patch keeps the horse more comfortable when ridden for a long time.

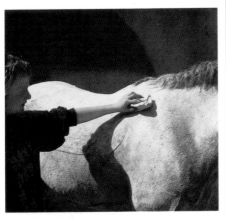

The blanket clip keeps a horse's back warm and avoids having to use several blankets in winter. Rubbing down with a warm damp cloth removes hair after clipping.

The full clip is used only on competition horses—when they finish competing they are very quickly covered with rugs to avoid chills.

LESSON 54 | **Teeth**

Check your horse's mouth regularly for bruising from the bit or cracked lips, which cause discomfort. Holding the tongue to one side lets you see the teeth.

Dental care is as important for horses as it is for people.

Horses with teeth or mouth problems cannot chew or digest food properly. A bridle may cause extra discomfort; the horse may object to having the bridle put on, or become difficult to ride.

The horse's jaw is wider on the top, meaning the teeth wear down unevenly with sharp edges on the molars—these cut the cheeks, especially in old horses. A horse dentist should visit twice a year to rasp any sharp edges, check teeth are in good condition, and that there are no infections.

Aging by teeth
The horse can be aged by its teeth fairly accurately up to the age of eight. After that,

1 year

Young horse or pony 8–10 years

Good horse dentists use a "gag" to hold the jaws apart to enable them to work without being nipped. Like a lot of people, some horses don't like the dentist!

The gag is removed once the worst of the edges are done and the rest are filed with a teeth rasp. Warm water with salt or antiseptic is used to clean out the mouth.

a rough estimate can be made by assessing the shape, degree of wear, and angle of the front teeth.

3 years

5 years

10 years

20–25 years

Middle-aged horse or pony 10–15 years

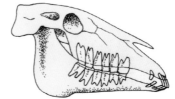

Old horse or pony 25 years

LESSON 55 | **Getting fit**

Controlled galloping up a gradual
slope or on sand is a popular form of further
fitness work—the horses really enjoy it.

Different horses require different levels of exercise.

A horse only ridden on weekends will need some form of exercise during the rest of the week. A horse that is competing regularly will require fitness work on a daily basis.

Like an athlete, a horse needs to be fit if it is going to perform to its best ability, and it cannot be expected to go from a life of leisure to one where it has to perform a specific role.

Start slowly, walking and trotting on good, consistent ground on roads and tracks to avoid slips and strains. Encourage the horse to use his muscles and don't let it dawdle.

After at least a month of slow fitness work, you can begin schooling for Dressage or jumping. Changes should be gradual and distances should be increased bit by bit. Make sure you don't bore the horse—always vary its work. It is important to adjust your horse's feed when you change his work rate.

SEE ALSO
Horse handling **page 106**
Schooling **page 108**
Fitness for competition **page 162**

LESSON 56 | **Winter care**

In winter, your horse requires extra shelter, warmth, and constant monitoring to avoid health problems.

If your horse is kept in half the time it is better to stable the horse at night and turn out during the day. If your horse is turned out all the time, you will notice it is too cold for it to rest at night; it keeps moving and grazing, then rests during the warmth of the day.

Warmbloods, Thoroughbreds, and Arabs will need extra food, since they use more energy to keep warm. Hardier breeds do not, but that won't stop a native pony from asking.

Shelter needs to be provided in the pasture—it should be open on the side away from the prevailing wind and have a hard floor, not mud.

In cold weather it may be necessary to break up ice to ensure that your horse can drink, or to take containers to the paddock.

Be aware of snow getting caught under the horse's shoes and forming balls of ice, on which your horse is likely to slip—it may also slip on ice on the road, or damage its legs cantering on frozen ground.

Watch out for health conditions such as lice (see page 177) and mud fever (see page 180).

Shetland ponies often have a layer of snow on their backs in the wild in winter—this shows how good their coat is at keeping the heat in, and the cold out. Horses that live out in the winter should not be clipped.

SEE ALSO
Horse rugs **page 68**
Feeds and feeding **page 142**
Clipping **page 148**

A waterproof New Zealand rug will help to keep the chills out—your horse will use up vital energy just to keep itself warm. Clipped horses may need a quilted rug underneath.

LESSON 57 | **Summer care**

Your horse requires different care in summer—here is a collection of warm-weather tips.

Stable the horse during the day and turn out at night to prevent overeating, summer itch, and sunburn to pale horses.

Shelter needs to be provided in the pasture—if the winter shelter does not provide shade all day in the summer, make sure your horse can get shade elsewhere.

Make sure the horse has clean fresh water. Containers in the paddock will quickly become stagnant and may become a midge breeding ground.

Keep the horse clean; it will sweat more at this time of year. Either let sweat dry and brush it off, or, if it is a warm day, wash the horse down.

Use fly repellent to give your horse peace in the paddock. If the horse has no tail for one reason or another, ensure it also has a fly mask.

Build work up gradually—it might be your summer holiday, but it isn't your horse's. Doing too much with an unfit horse may cause lameness lasting all holiday.

Watch out for health conditions such as summer itch (see page 177) and laminitis (see page 183).

SEE ALSO
Grooming essentials **page 86**
Getting fit **page 152**

COMPETITION HORSE CARE

This section details the changes you will need to make to your horse's care for successful competition, plus a section dedicated to loading and transporting your horse.

LESSON 58 | Competition feeding

A competition horse requires special feed to maintain condition when training; it must be steadily built up along with workload, and cut on rest days.

Vitamins A, B1, B2, B6, D, and E are all essential to horse health; if the horse looks out of condition, consult the vet. A vitamin deficiency can be remedied by supplementing the diet with extra vitamins. Most feed mixes will have added vitamins and minerals in the correct amount and balance, they will include most of those adequate to keep your animal in peak condition. It should not be necessary to feed supplements.

Competition horse feed guide

	Morning	Evening
Rest	None	2.2 lb (1 kg) 12% protein mix
Light work	2.2 lb (1 kg) 14% protein mix	2.2 lb (1 kg) mix + 1.1lb (0.5 kg) chaff
Medium work	3.3 lb (1.5 kg) mix	3.3 lb (1.5 kg) mix + 1.1lb (0.5 kg) chaff
Hard work	3.85 lb (1.75 kg) mix	3.85 lb (1.75 kg) mix + 1.1lb (0.5 kg) chaff

SEE ALSO
Feeds and feeding **page 142**
Getting fit **page 152**

Suggested ratios of hay to concentrate foods

Rest days	100% hay or grass
Light work	85% hay: 15% concentrates
Medium work	75% hay: 25% concentrates
Hard work	65% hay: 35% concentrates

Always ensure you leave enough time after feeding before starting work to avoid colic (see page 183).

Competition horses require a special diet to keep them going through intensive training.

LESSON 59 | **Competition grooming**

A braided mane and tail show off your horse to its best advantage and are regarded as part of a neat turn-out.

The starting point is a well-pulled mane and full tail; do not shampoo them first because this makes the hair too slippery to braid neatly. Decide on a style; thick necks look finer with neat braids pulled down into the crest, while larger braids on top enhance weak necks. Several styles are illustrated on these pages.

Braided tail

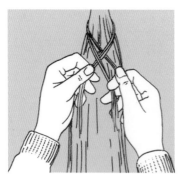

1 Take sections from both sides, including an even amount of hair from each side.

2 Braid down center for two-thirds of dock, keeping the hairs evenly spaced.

3 The finished tail looks neat with the actual braid kept central on the tail.

SEE ALSO
Grooming essentials **page 86**
Extended grooming kit **page 89**

English braids

1 Split the mane into equal sections. Damp a section, then split into three even sections and braid together tightly.

2 Secure the end with rubber bands or matching thread. Fold up twice and secure on top of the neck.

3 After completing all the braids down the neck, finish by braiding the forelock, taking care to keep it straight.

Continental braids

1 Divide the mane into even sections as in English braiding. Braid tightly and loop the mane up once.

2 Leave a 1–1 ½ inch (2.5–4 cm) loop of mane and secure with thread or rubber bands.

3 Take white tape and wind around the braid, leaving a neat bud of mane showing at the end.

LESSON 59 | **Competition grooming** continued

Different mane and tail styles suit different horses—choose something that enhances your horse's shape and character.

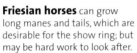

Friesian horses can grow long manes and tails, which are desirable for the show ring; but may be hard work to look after.

Continental braids are eye-catching when used with white numnahs.

Arabs and other horses with high tail carriage will look far better with a full tail.

A full mane and tail keeps this pony warm, and they are trimmed straight for neatness.

This Arabian, running, or gypsy braid is for horses with unusually long flowing manes.

LESSON 60 | **Fitness for competition**

This lesson concentrates on readying a horse for eventing, in many ways the peak of fitness of a horse.

Before doing any serious training, it is vital that at least one month should be spent conditioning the horse's muscles before it is required to do anything more strenuous.

Leg protection when training over varied ground is a must: well-fitting boots that do not rub and over-reach boots when galloping or cross-country schooling. A small cut or bruise may develop, with maddening consequences. Don't forget studs in hard or slippery conditions to give a better grip.

Jumping training should build athleticism and balance—school regularly to teach agility over poles and fences at home, and also over a variety of cross-country fences. You will need to be able to jump at speed, maintaining balance and control.

SEE ALSO
Schooling **page 108** Eventing **page 124**
Lunging **page 110**   Getting fit **page 152**
Dressage **page 120**

Galloping is done once or twice a week and develops breathing capacity by exercising the lungs. Interval training starts with three three-minute canters, separated by three-minute walking periods. Gradually increase canter time and decrease walking.

Practice the test during the last couple of weeks before the first competition—only do the entire test a couple of times otherwise your horse may start to anticipate. Make sure you are both confident about the movements required. Ride individual exercises and ensure the whole test is committed to memory.

Many horses who become idle on their own work much better in company, as do riders, during the laborious fitness work.

LESSON 61 | **Transportation**

The transportation of horses requires planning, however short the journey.

Generally, problems arise only if the horse is swung too fast around corners and finds difficulty in maintaining its balance, or if the brakes are applied too violently. Horses do not suffer from travel sickness, but some are nervous travelers, and may need sedation to prevent injury.

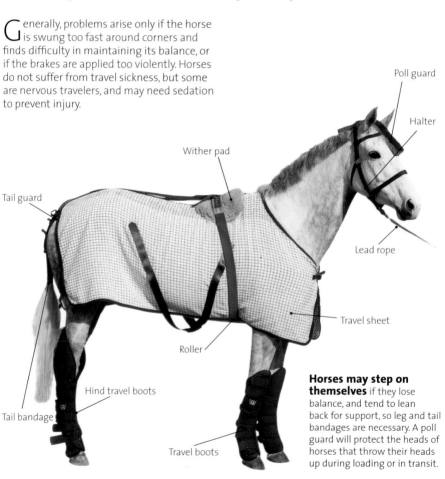

Poll guard

Halter

Wither pad

Tail guard

Lead rope

Travel sheet

Roller

Tail guard

Hind travel boots

Tail bandage

Travel boots

Horses may step on themselves if they lose balance, and tend to lean back for support, so leg and tail bandages are necessary. A poll guard will protect the heads of horses that throw their heads up during loading or in transit.

Vehicle preparation

The vehicle must be safe and roadworthy with correctly pressured tires for the load. The ramp must be secure and all fixtures must be in good working order so that the horse is properly contained. Horses will appreciate a hay net during the journey, and a stop for a drink of water every two hours.

A two-horse trailer of a type popular in Europe. Use partitions even when traveling with only one horse, since they help to keep the horse balanced.

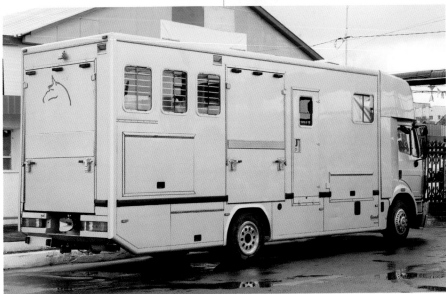

SEE ALSO
Horse rugs **page 68**
Boots and bandages **page 72**

A competition box, with rear and side loading, space for three horses, and a living compartment for the rider to change and sleep in. Note the storage hatches—these can be used to store feed or bulky kit.

LESSON 62 | **Loading**

Horses may be frightened of entering
a trailer for the first time. Patience
and practice is the key—try loading with
another horse or encouraging it with food.

1 Be confident and walk toward the horse box in a positive attitude. Keep the horse straight and allow it time to adjust to walking up the ramp.

2 Make sure you give the horse enough room to turn into its compartment once you reach the top of the ramp. You may need to go on ahead to allow it to turn.

SEE ALSO
Horse handling **page 106**
Transportation **page 164**

3 Untie the horse before opening the partition. Do not hurry; the horse may need a few minutes to adjust to the light and new surroundings.

4 Allow the horse to take one step at a time and come down steadily to avoid slips or stumbles. If reversing out, keep straight and give the horse time to adjust to his surroundings.

LESSON 63 | **Vet checks**

In competition, horses as well as riders are checked for fitness before being allowed to compete, and winning horses are also routinely drug tested in most sports.

In other sports, such as endurance riding, the final condition of the horse forms part of the total mark.

On the last day of a three-day event, horses must pass the final horse inspection, designed to ensure they are still fit to showjump after the demands of the cross country. It is one of the most nerve-racking moments for the event rider since failure results in elimination from the competition. The horse must also pass inspections before the event begins and during the cross country.

SEE ALSO
Eventing **page 124**
Lameness **page 181**

The horse is "trotted up" to check for lameness. It should be gently hacked out and then do ten minutes of loosening work before the inspection. Keep the horse in a good rhythm and ensure its head is straight so that it takes even steps. Its legs will be felt for heat, and its overall condition checked.

Time out
It is important to give competition horses time away from their gruelling training to relax and gallop with other horses.

HORSE HEALTH

Disease prevention is an essential part of an owner's responsibility, and tetanus, equine infectious anaemia, and equine flu immunization should be routine precautions. It is helpful to compile a disease-control program for your horse, and to enter the dates when the various procedures are due on a calendar or year planner.

In this chapter, information is given on a range of the most common ailments of the horse, and how to prevent, detect, and treat them. By preventing disease and treating simple injuries yourself you can save on vets bills—but if in doubt, it is always worth consulting your vet.

Healthy hooves
The farrier (left) is as important as the vet to the ongoing health of your horse.

LESSON 64 | **The healthy horse**

A healthy horse is bright, alert, and in good body condition. Getting to know your horse and its usual behavior will help you to judge when it is feeling off-color.

A healthy and reasonably fit horse— you should always see a shine in the coat, unless the coat is dirty.

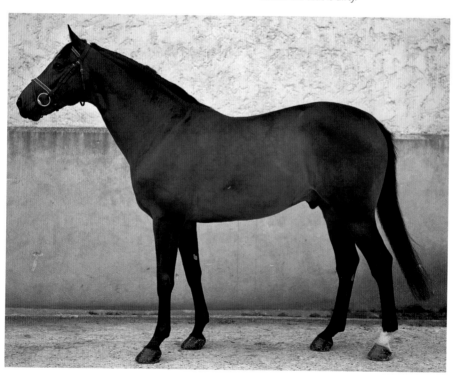

Horses normally stand during the daytime; if lying down when approached they should get up quickly and stand evenly on all four feet.

Droppings should be passed about eight times a day and should be a damp ball that just breaks up on contact with the ground. The color of droppings depends on the diet—they are looser when the animal is in pasture. Urine should be pale yellow, fairly thick, and passed several times a day.

A neglected horse—thin, lame, and with sores. Note the dull coat—grooming will not make any difference here.

Horse health checklist

Coat Flat and shiny (not winter coat).

Skin Supple, easily moved over flesh.

Eyes Bright, lining membrane salmon pink.

Gums and nostrils Salmon-pink color.

Limbs Free from heat and swelling.

Ribs will show on a fit horse—spine should not.

Strides Equal length, weight evenly distributed.

Eats well and chews food properly.

Breathing Even and regular, eight to twelve times per minute at rest.

Sweat Should not at rest.

Temperature 101.5° Fahrenheit (35°C).

Pulse 36 to 42 a minute at rest.

LESSON 65 | **Choosing a vet**

If you are registered, you can get phone advice or a vet in an emergency easily.

It is always difficult to know when to seek professional help. As a rule, it is better to do this sooner rather than later—delay, in many conditions, may have serious consequences. Where there is any doubt, it is best to contact the vet, giving him or her as many details as possible (whether the horse is off its food, has a temperature, is sweating, or is behaving abnormally), discussing with him or her whether or not a visit is necessary and what you should do until the vet arrives. For cases of colic, the vet should be called immediately. The sooner painkillers are administered, the less chance there is of complications. Horses with a fever—a temperature of more than 101.5° Fahrenheit (38.6°C) also need veterinary attention, as do those suffering from acute lameness or injury. To have a chance of healing successfully following stitching, wounds must be treated when fresh. Accordingly, it is important to call a vet as soon as a cut is discovered—there is little point in asking the vet to stitch it on the following day (see also page 185).

Tips to find a vet

- Ask other horse owners which vet they use.
- Some vets specialize—check they treat horses.
- Will the vet visit for check-ups at a suitable time for you?
- Call-out fees are expensive—can you ride there for vaccinations?
- Ask for prices to compare vets.
- What is the emergency service?
- Do they operate on horses, if not, where will you be referred?
- The receptionists/nurses should be friendly and knowledgeable.
- The building should be reasonably clean.
- You should trust them, and so should your horse.

Regular checks

Your horse will need to have various vaccinations and checks periodically. The most common are listed here, however different countries have different regulations, so check requirements with your new vet.

- **Tetanus booster** Two years— worldwide requirement.
- **Vet general health check** Every 12 months or when vaccinating.
- **Equine flu booster** 11 to 12 months— must have for competitive horses, and may be a requirement for livery yards (see page 43).
- **Dentist** 6 months (see page 150).
- **Worming** 6 to 10 weeks (see page 176).
- **Farrier** 4 to 6 weeks (see page 146).
- **You** Every day. Watch for changes in behavior that may indicate illness— see the next few pages for more information on specific illnesses.

LESSON 66 | **Common ailments**

Your horse relies on you to recognize when it is sick. Illness can happen at any time, and you need to have a basic knowledge of the symptoms. Always call a vet if you have any doubts.

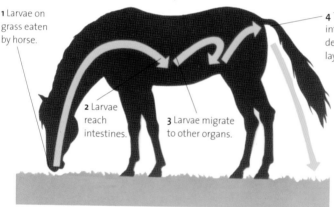

1 Larvae on grass eaten by horse.

2 Larvae reach intestines.

3 Larvae migrate to other organs.

4 They return to intestines and develop into egg-laying worms.

Life cycle of the large redworm, the most damaging equine parasite.

Parasites

Parasites are creatures that live on and in your horse, stealing the nutrients from their feed, drinking their blood, and generally making the horse feel miserable.

Worms are a fact of life for most grazing animals, but especially domesticated horses, because they are restricted to feeding repeatedly on the same pasture. All horses carry a certain amount of worms. It is when they become excessive that they cause damage to the digestive system and internal organs. If untreated, the horse could seriously lose condition and even die.

To prevent this, your horse must be wormed regularly; talk to your vet about the most effective treatment and the frequency with which you will need to dose. It is important to keep your muck heap several yards from the edge of the paddock, and to collect droppings from the grass periodically if grazing is restricted.

Bots are the larvae of gadflies, which worry horses during the hot weather. Gadflies "cement" their eggs onto the horse's coat—often on the legs—which are then licked up. The larvae burrow into the mucous membranes of the mouth and then migrate to the stomach.

It is a sensible precaution to use a wormer that is known to be effective against bots at least twice a year. Remove clumps of yellow eggs from the horse's legs in late summer with a hard dandy brush. If infestation is very heavy, clip the legs to remove all the eggs.

Heel bug is the larval stage of the harvest mite; it is red in color and also sucks blood from humans. During harvest, the mites end up in straw bales; when the horse is bedded down on infected straw, the mites bite and cause intense irritation. If suspected, change the bedding, and wash the legs in an insecticidal shampoo.

Lice are quite common in horses in winter. Lice can usually be seen moving in the coat—they are white or yellowish in color and are about the size of a pinhead. They provoke intense itching and an infected horse will rub its skin bald. Use an insecticidal shampoo or louse powder—as this is a winter condition, when washing the horse you must be careful not to cause scratches (see page 179).

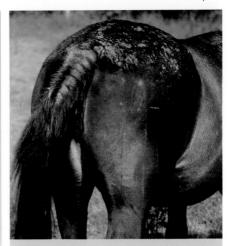

Typical summer-itch damage—the tail takes a while to grow back. Bandaging may help if caught early on—you may have to "hog" (cut off) the mane if it is patchy.

Summer itch is caused by an allergy to the saliva of midges. Affected animals suffer intense irritation, and most of the damage is from itching. This causes loss of hair and raw sores on the root of the tail, on the withers, and up the neck.

It is a difficult condition to treat once begun, often requiring injections to break the itch–scratch cycle. The best course of action is to prevent the allergic horse from being bitten by midges. Horses should be stabled from mid-afternoon until the following morning. Windows and openings above the stall door should be fitted with fine-mesh screens, and the horse treated with fly repellents. Rugs, fly masks, and neck coverings are also very useful.

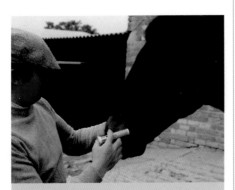

Wormers are supplied as paste in tubes, and are easy to use.

LESSON 66 | **Common ailments** continued

A case of thrush caused by droppings and wet bedding left in the foot—you must pick out the horse's feet every day.

Bacteria and fungi

Bacteria and fungi cause various unsightly and painful infections and skin complaints—these are often highly infectious, and can be spread by sharing grooming kit.

Ringworm in horses is usually acquired by direct contact with another infected horse or through infected tack or grooming kit, although it is possible for them to catch the cattle version. There is an incubation period of five to ten days, before small, rounded patches appear. These enlarge and small fluid-filled vesicles form, which may rupture and form scabs.

Isolate the infected horse and all its kit until he is clear of the fungi. Topical fungicides can be used on the spots, and tack and grooming equipment should be cleaned with a disinfectant that specifically kills fungi. If the horse is very badly infected it may need a systemic fungicide by mouth.

Rain rot and grease are caused by a bacteria, which can only grow in continual damp and the absence of oxygen. Rain rot develops under the thick, matted coats of the hindquarters in winter. The infection is in the skin under the matted hair, beneath a thick scab. The matted hair and scab can be removed—if it is not a huge area—killing the bacteria, and a cream can then be applied.

On the lower legs it is known as "grease" and can be scrubbed off using an antibacterial shampoo. In severe infections, or when the legs swell, antibiotics may be needed. The horse must be stabled and kept clean and dry until the infection has cleared up.

Other skin complaints

Scratches are formed when the skin above the heels becomes reddened, tender, and scaly. Later, small fluid-filled vesicles develop, which rupture, and cracks appear across the skin. These may ooze serum that dries on the surface, but the wounds often crack again when the animal moves. The horse may become lame. Secondary infection may spread up the leg.

Legs with white markings get scratches more often; probably because they are usually caused by washing the legs in cold weather. Allow mud to dry, then brush off instead. Wash affected legs with medicated shampoo and dry thoroughly, before applying soothing ointment on a piece of lint and bandaging to the leg. Reapplication prevents repeated cracking of the wound, delaying healing.

Cracked heels and mud fever are caused by damp or muddy conditions, which make the skin soft and sore. Any cracks that develop can quickly become infected if not treated, causing lameness or soreness and swelling.

Horses with white legs or feather are more prone—clip away excess hair and apply barrier creams to prevent problems. Use a kaolin poultice to clean up sores before treating with antibiotic or barrier cream. Keep the area dry and free of dirt.

Thrush is an easy-to-detect infection of the foot, where the frog (see page 16) becomes foul smelling and appears moist. Treatment consists of thorough cleaning and spraying with antibiotic spray. Beds should always be kept as clean and dry as possible—thrush only occurs in horses kept in poor conditions.

Girth galls are caused by the girth rubbing on sensitive skin. They are particularly common on horses that have just come back to work after a rest, when the skin is soft and the hair often long and dirty. Hard or dirty girths can also be a cause. Treat with poultices and do not ride until better. Clean the girth area well before riding and harden the skin with salt water or surgical spirit unless it is broken. A girth sleeve and soft well-oiled girths will help to prevent it.

Saddle sores are caused by pressure or friction from badly fitting tack. Get your tack checked by an expert—barrel-shaped horses may require a breastplate or crupper to hold the saddle in position, or a thick, soft numnah under the saddle may help. (See pages 50–77 for info on tack)

Allergic skin reactions to feed or change of diet will settle within 24 hours, although severe cases may need antihistamines. Sometimes, a bran mash made with Epsom

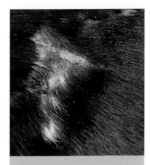

Saddle sores are treated by daily application of a wound care (consult your vet). You must not ride the horse until the sores have healed.

LESSON 66 | **Common ailments** continued

Bruises from everyday work are best treated with cold hosing for ten minutes, two or three times a day, to relieve inflammation. After 48 hours of cold treatment, hot poultices or warm dry bandaging create extra circulation to disperse bruising. The more the animal can move about, the better it will be.

salts can help. A change in diet might have been introduced too suddenly or the horse could be reacting to a fly bite. Some animals are sun sensitive and may need to be kept in during the day and turned out only at night.

Corns are caused by pressure creating bruising under the shoe. Bruising should be cut out so that it does not build up. Some corns go septic, requiring a poultice to draw out the inflammation before the shoe can be replaced. The farrier will treat this, possibly with special shoes.

Over-reach is caused by the back foot over-extending and clipping the front one, and is particularly common when jumping, on deep ground, or when galloping. This can cause a nasty bruise, or a deep cut on the front heel. Over-reach bell boots will protect the heels (see page 73).

Brushing is caused by the one foot passing too close to the opposite leg, and can result in nasty cuts and bruises from the edges of the shoe. Brushing boots will prevent further injuries (see page 73). As with over-reaching, it is more likely during competition.

Filled legs are usually caused by of overfeeding and under-exercising. It is usually noticeable in the hindlegs first, then all four. Check your food/work program and try cutting down the food a little, especially if the horse is in good condition. A bran mash may help to clear out any excess proteins. The filling usually disappears with exercise. If in doubt, consult the veterinarian.

If you have done more exercise than usual—a long trek, or more galloping— you may see filling caused by jarring of the legs. Some cold hosing and quiet walking should help.

Splints are caused by working on hard ground, a direct blow, or by too much work with a young horse. They are a small, hard lump of new bone growth, usually on the cannon bones, just below the knee or hock.

Treatment consists of rest and cold hosing to reduce inflammation. Rest and anti-inflammatory drugs may be necessary for up to six weeks until the splint has hardened.

Navicular disease is chronic foreleg lameness, usually affecting both limbs. The onset is generally gradual, and the horse may start out slightly lame, but become sound during exercise. The disease usually develops in horses that are five to eight years old and is practically unknown in ponies.

In navicular disease there is a decreased blood flow within the navicular bone inside the hoof. Because of lack of blood, the navicular bone thins and blood channels enlarge, both of which can be seen on X-ray examination. Until recently, navicular disease was incurable, however symptoms are now successfully relieved with drug regimes in about 80 percent of cases. Surgical shoeing is also very useful.

Lameness

Care of the legs is vital if your horse is to stay sound throughout its career. Ignoring what seems like a minor ailment today, could cause greater problems in the future.

Keep your horse shod regularly, never overwork your horse, look for warning signs, such as inflammation or heat, and act quickly so they do not worsen.

CHECKING FOR LAMENESS
Ask someone to trot the horse on a level surface. Keep a loose lead rein to allow free head movement. If the horse's head stays level, it is sound in front. If lame, its head will nod down with the good front leg, and up as the lame one goes down. Depth of nod indicates the degree of lameness. Hindleg lameness is more difficult; you will need to watch the quarters. The horse will drop on to one side and raise the other.

FINDING THE PROBLEM
1 Get an overall impression by feeling down the whole leg from the top. Look at it from all angles.

2 If the problem is in the foot, the hoof may feel warm and a pulse may be felt in the heel.

3 Lift the foot up and ensure there is nothing stuck in the foot. If there is—remove it.

LAMENESS WITH AGE
Some older horses will come out stiff behind if they have been in a stable for 24 hours, but should be fine after five minutes of walking.

As the horse gets older, it may develop arthritis in the same way as humans. Talk to your veterinarian, who will probably prescribe an anti-inflammatory drug to

LESSON 66 | **Common ailments** continued

Trotting up
This horse has a showy trot and is obviously not lame.

relieve any pain or stiffness. Do not over-exert your horse, though gentle exercise may help to prevent the condition worsening. The cold weather aggravates arthritis, so keep the horse warm and bandage its legs in very cold weather.

Spinal lameness may cause uneven gaits, sinking down when mounting, and crooked jumping. An awkward landing while jumping is the usual cause, resulting in pulled muscles or the spine and pelvis being slightly out of line. Gentle pressure from two or three fingers worked systematically down on either side of the spine may indicate where the problem is.

Laminitis is a severe condition causing inflammation of the feet. Because the hoof cannot expand, the pain caused by the swelling is excruciating and causes severe distress. The horse will lean back to get the weight off its front feet and will be reluctant to move. The vet should be called.

The cause is usually dietary, particularly a sudden change in diet or rich grass. A laxative diet and cooling of the feet by hosing or standing in a river may ease discomfort. Painkillers will be required in severe cases. Fat ponies are particularly prone and should be kept on restricted grazing in spring.

Serious ailments

Chronic obstructive pulmonary disease (COPD) is particularly common among stabled horses, where sensitivity to dust and spores develops into a cough with thick mucus. Left untreated, the horse will gradually deteriorate. Provide as much fresh air as possible, bed on paper or shavings, and soak hay or feed haylage. Keep the horse out in a paddock, and ask the vet about dilators and expectorants for more serious cases.

Equine flu is a highly infectious disease causing high temperature, cough, and nasal discharge. The horse may also go off its feed. Isolation from other horses and rest are required. Cut down grain in feed, but keep up the roughage, such as hay, and provide plenty of fresh water. It will take two or three weeks for the horse to recover, so gradual work can commence. Regular vaccinations will help to prevent severe cases, even if they do not cover all strains of the virus (these are mandatory for competitive horses).

Azoturia makes the horse's muscles—particularly along the back and quarters—go into spasm. It may start as stiffness, then the horse will suddenly slow up as the muscles spasm, start to sweat, and become distressed. Cease exercise immediately and keep the horse warm. Take off the saddle or loosen the girth. Arrange transport home if the horse is very still, as further exercise can do more damage. Once home, rest the horse and give a laxative diet with Epsom salts. Get a vet to take a blood sample to determine the severity of the attack, which will then establish a timeframe for the horse's gradual return to work.

Tetanus or **lockjaw** is usually fatal so vaccination of all horses is vital. Puncture wounds allow bacteria from the soil to enter the horse's system; ask the vet about boosters after injuries. The disease initially causes muscle stiffness, then the third eyelid closes across the eye, jaw movements become restricted, and paralysis set in.

Strangles is a severe and highly infectious bacterial disease of the air passages in the throat. It causes large abscesses, which burst internally or externally and affect breathing and swallowing. The horse may have a very high temperature, a thick nasal discharge, and be extremely miserable.

Strict isolation procedures must be implemented immediately; all affected bedding will have to be burned and the whole area thoroughly disinfected. Equipment and clothing must be disinfected, as will the hands and feet of people in contact with the horse. Antibiotics will be given after the abscesses have burst. Feed the horse from the floor while it is ill. Apply hot fomentations to the throat area and bathe the eyes and nostrils as often. The vet will take blood to determine when the horse is free of infection.

Colic is abdominal pain usually caused by a change in the diet, dehydration, worms, over feeding, or kidney problems. It is potentially very serious, and can lead to death.

The horse becomes very restless, looking around at its stomach and kicking at it. It may sweat, and breathing and pulse rate increase. If it does not settle after 20 minutes, or if the horse becomes violent, or is in obvious pain, call the vet immediately. Do not allow the horse to roll, as this may cause a twist in the intestines, which may be fatal. Keep the horse moving, and keep it warm.

LESSON 67 | **First aid for horses**

Put horses and people together and there is always bound to be the odd bruise, knock, or fall.

No matter how confident you are around horses, they can still be unpredictable. Just as often, the fault is the rider's, with complacency leading to carelessness.

Horse first aid kit

- **Cotton wool.**
- **Container for bathing wounds.**
- **Kaolin.**
- **Poultices.**
- **Scissors for cutting dressings.**
- **Sterile non-stick dressings.**
- **Salt or antiseptic solution.**
- **Bandages or leg wraps to hold dressings in place and for dry bandaging.**
- **Instant "cold" packs for reducing inflammation.**
- **Antiseptic wound spray and powder.**
- **Thermometer.**

SEE ALSO
Boots and bandages **page 72**

Before providing first aid of any kind, work through these steps:

- Move uninjured people/horses away from the accident.

- Secure the site of the accident: if on a road, stop the car; switch off electricity, water, or machinery; and close gates or doors to contain the injured horse.

- Call the vet and/or ambulance for life-threatening injuries.

- Tie injured horses up since they can become dangerous because of pain.

- Never give first aid if doing so would put you in physical danger.

Deciding when to call the vet can be difficult. The easiest way to decide is to think of yourself with the same symptoms: would you go to the doctors? If you would, then the horse needs the vet. If you wouldn't, then you will probably be able to treat your horse with a bit of common sense.

Bruises and swellings may inflame quickly or come up gradually. The sooner you can apply ice or a cold pack to the area the better—a packet of frozen peas makes an easy substitute.

Bandage ice packs over gauze to prevent skin scalding. Replace hourly, for up to four

hours, then hose with cold water two or three times daily for minor bruises. For large bruises hose for 10 to 20 minutes every two hours. The first 24 hours are most important to reduce swelling.

Serious cuts can be lightly hosed or left and covered with a non-stick dressing. The flow of blood will help clean the wound, but bleeding should stop after a few minutes. Place a dressing over the wound and apply pressure. Leave the last applied dressing on the wound (in case it is stuck to a scab) and apply a bandage until the vet arrives.

Cut arteries are life threatening—they spurt blood in heartbeat bursts, and if not stopped the horse may bleed out. Call a vet immediately. Apply a pad and a bandage or firm pressure, and keep adding dressings if bleeding persists. Keep the horse still and quiet.

As rider and horse face more difficult challenges as the level of riding increases, it may be said that so does the likelihood of having an accident.

A tourniquet should be applied only if the arterial cut is imminently life threatening. Apply over the wound or just above, between the heart and the wound. Tourniquets must be loosened every 10 to 15 minutes to prevent circulation problems.

Puncture wounds can be dangerous and it is much safer to get the vet to ensure the wound is thoroughly cleaned inside. Antibiotics may be prescribed and your vet will check your horse is covered against tetanus.

A picture of health
Maintaining your horse's health will allow
a long and exciting partnership to flourish.

INDEX

A

aging by teeth 150–151
aids 96–99
allergies 45, 177, 179–180
American Quarter Horse 10
American Saddlebred 10, 23
anti-sweat sheet 71
Appaloosa 10
Arab 6, 11, 161
arteries, cut 185
auction sales 35
Australian tack 67
azoturia 183

B

back (flexor) tendons 15
back protector 83
balance 109
bandages 72, 74–75
bar 16
barbed wire 46
bareback riding 109, 133
barn system 41
barrel racing 116, 134–135
Bay 18
bedding 44–45, 139
behavioral science 28–29
Belgian Draught horse 126
bits 57
Black 19
black points 14
blanket clip 149
blaze 20
blind spots 28
blinkers 28
Blue Roan 18
body language 24–25
bolting 29
boots (for horse) 72–73, 164
boots (for rider) 78, 79, 83
    cowboy boots 84, 85
boredom 30

bosal 62
bots 176–177
braids 159–161
branding 48
breaking in 34
breast 15
breathing 16, 173
breeches 78
breeds 10–11
bridles 57
    cleaning 76
    leading with 107
    one-eared 62
    slip-eared 63
    Western 62–63, 66, 67
bridling 59
brisket 15
bronco riding 133
Brown 18
bruises and swellings 181,
    184–185
brushing 180
brushing boots 72–73
brushing rings 73
bulb 15, 16
buttock 14
buying a horse 32–35

C

cannon 14, 15
canter 22, 23, 99
    counter canter 99
    Western riding 105
cantle 52, 60
catching a horse 107
chaps 78, 79, 83, 84, 85
cheek bone 15
chest 15
Chestnut (color) 18
chestnut (point) 15
chewing (vice) 30, 31
Cheyenne roll 60

chin groove 15
chronic obstructive
    pulmonary disease 183
cinch 60
claustrophobia 29
clippers 89
clipping 148–149, 154
clothing see riding gear
Clydesdale 6, 11, 20
coffin bone 16
cold bloods 6
colic 174, 183
collected trot 121
collection 22
colors and markings 18–21
combinations 122, 124
communication 24–5, 26
companion animals 29,
    36–37, 43
competitive riding 117–135
    competition feeding 156–157
    competition grooming
        158–161
    fitness 162–163
    shoe studs 147
corn, seat of 16
corns 180
coronary band 16
coronet 14
cracked heels 179
Cream 19
crest 15
crib biting 30, 31
cribbing 30
cross country 80, 124
    eventing 124
    fences 125
cross poles 113
croup 14
crupper 55
currycombing 88, 141
cutting 132

D

dandy brushing 88, 140
Dapple Gray 19
Dartmoor 8
dead-sides 97
dealers 35
deep litter 45
dentists 151, 175
dismounting
   European 95
   Western 100–101
distance, ability to judge
   28, 29
dock 14, 141
double bridle 57
Dressage 20, 119, 120–121
   eventing 124
   riding gear 79, 81,
      120–121
   saddle 53
   tack 51
drop jumps 125
drop noseband 56

E

ears, body language 25
eggbutt snaffle 57
elbow 15
equine flu 175, 183
equipment 38–42
   insurance 48
ergot 15
European style riding
   93–99
   aids 96–99
   mounting and
      dismounting 94–95
   paces 98–99
eventing 124, 125
exercise sheet 71
extended trot 121
extension 22

eyes 173
   body language 25
   cleaning 141
   vision 28–29

F

farriers 146–7, 170, 175
feeds and feeding 142–145,
   154, 181–182
   competition feeding
      156–157
   storage 41
   supplements 145
fences 122, 125
fencing 46, 48, 49
fender 60
fetlock 14, 15
filled legs 180–181
finger brushing 141
fire hazard 41, 48
first aid kit 184
fitness 152–153, 162–163
flank 14
flank strap 60
flash noseband 56
Fleabitten Gray 19
flexor tendons 15
fly mask 155, 177
flying change 99, 105
foreleg brushing boots 72
forelock 15
Friesian 11, 160
frog 16

G

gadflies 176
gaits see paces
gallop 16, 22, 23, 99
gaskin 14
gates, situating 46
girth 52, 54, 58
girth galls 179
gloves 79

grackle 56
Gray 19
grazing 46–47
grease 178
grooming 140–141, 155
   competition grooming
      158–161
   grass-kept horses 86
   kit 86–89, 178
grooming mitt 89
gymkhanas 118, 119

H

hackamore 57
hacking jacket 79
half pass 97, 121
halt 97
halter, leading with 106
hamstring 14
hand aids 97
handling 106–107
hands (measurement) 17
hay nets 143
head, throwing 29
health checklist
   172–173
hedging 46
heel bug 177
herd instinct 29, 36–37
hindleg brushing
   boots 73
hindquarters 14
hobble strap 60
hock 14
hock boots 72
hoof oil 89
hoof pick 88
hoofbrands 48
hooves 14, 16, 171
   picking 87
   shoeing 146–147
   trimming 146

horn 60
horse whisperers 26, 111
hunter clip 149
hurdles 129

I
insect bites 69, 155, 177
insurance 48
itch blanket 69

J
jodhpurs 79
jog 104
Join Up method 26
jugular groove 15
jump saddle 53
jumping 40–41, 109
    lunging over jumps 111

K
kicking 29, 55
kimblewick curb 57
knee caps 72

L
lameness 181–182
laminae 16
laminitis 155, 182
leading 106–107
leg aids 97, 109
leg markings 20, 21
lice 154, 177
Liver Chestnut 18
livery 43
loading 166
lockjaw 183
loins 14
long reining 111
loose-ring snaffle 57
lope 105
lunging 110–111
lungs 16

M
mane 15, 161
    braids 159–161
markings see colors and
    markings
measuring the horse 17
microchip implants 48
mockers 79
Morgan 11
mounting
    European 94
    Western 100–101
mounting block 94
mucking out 138–139
mud fever 154, 179
Mustang 12
muzzle 15

N
navicular disease 181
New Forest Pony 12
New Zealand blanket 71, 154
Norwegian Fjord 6–7
nosebands 56
numnah 52, 55, 58

O
Odd Colored 19
Olympics 93
overreach 180
overreach boots 73

P
paces 22–3
    European 98–99
    Western 104–105
Paint horse 19
Palomino 19, 131
parasites 176–177
passage, the 121
passports 21
pastern 14, 15

pastern bones
    long 16
    short 16
pasture 46–47, 143, 145
pawing 31
peat moss 45
pedal bone 16
petal bell boots 73
Pinto 19
plain cavesson 56
plantar cushion 16
pleasure classes 130
points of the horse 14–16
poles 113
poll 15
poll guard 164
polo 127
pommel 52, 60
pony 17
Pony of the Americas 12, 17
Pony Club 118–119
Przewalski's horse 6
pulse 173

Q
quick release knot 139

R
racing 114–115, 128–129
rack 22, 23
rain rot 178
reigning (show class) 131
reigning back 97, 105
reins
    Californian 63
    Texan 63
respiration 16
ribs 15
riding gear 78–81
    Dressage 79, 81, 120–121
    safety gear 78, 79, 82–83
    Western 84–85

ringworm 178
road, riding on 29, 107
Roberts, Monty 26
rodeo riding 132–133
rollback 105
rugs and rugging
    up 68–71
running martingale 54

S
saddle sores 179
saddles 51–55
    Australian 67
    cleaning 77
    fitting 52
    Western 60–61, 64
saddling 58
safety
    riding gear 82–83
    stabling 48
safety helmet 78, 79, 81
schooling 108–109
schoolmaster 32
scratches 179
seat 96
security measures 48
Selle Français 12
serpentines 108, 109
shade, provision 155
sheets 70, 71
shelter, provision
    46, 154
Shetland 13, 154
Shire 6, 13, 20
shoeing 146–7
Show horses,
    markings 20
show jumping 81, 119,
    122, 123
    eventing 124
showing 118
Shy Boy 26

sliding stop 105, 131
snaffles 57
snip 21
snow and ice 154
sole 16
spin 105
spinal lameness 182
splints 181
stable blanket 70
stable yards 41
stables 29, 31, 40
    barn system 41
    bedding 44–45
    cleanliness 44, 138
    design 41, 42
    equipment
        40–41, 42
    flooring 41
    livery 43
    loosebox 42
    mucking out
        138–139
stall walking 31
stance 24
standing stalls 40
star 21
steeplechasing 129
steer wrestling 133
stifle 14, 15
stirrups 52, 54–55
strangles 183
straw bedding
    44–45
Strawberry Roan 18
stress 24, 29, 30, 31
stripe 20
summer 155
summer itch 155, 177
surcingles 68
sweat scraper 89
sweating 148, 155, 173
swell 60

T
tack 50–57
    Australian 67
    buying 50–51
    cleaning 76–77
    Dressage 51
    Western 60–64
tacking up 58–59
    Western 64–67
tail 14, 161
    body language 24
    braided 158
tail bandage 74,
    75, 141
tail guard 164
tapaderos 61
teeth 150–151
temperature 173
tendon boots 73
tetanus 175, 183
tethering 138, 139
theft, precautions
    against 48
Thoroughbred 13
throat 15
thrush 87, 178, 179
trace clipping 149
trail classes 130
Trakehner 13
transportation 164–166
travel wear 72, 75
traveling boots 72
tread cover 60
treats, feeding 107
trot 22, 98
turning left 97

U
under blanket 71

V
vaccinations 175

vaulting 126
vets 167, 171, 174–175
vices 30–31
vision 28–29

W
walk 22, 98, 104
wall 16
water jumps 125
water supply 143, 155
weaving 31
Western style riding
   92, 93
   bridles 62–63,
      66, 67
   clothing 84–5
   mounting and
      dismounting 100–101
   paces 104–105
   saddles 60–61, 64
   show classes 130–131

tacking up 64–67
   trainers 111
white face 20
white line 16
white markings
   20–21
wild horse racing 133
windpipe 15
winter 154
wither pad 164
withers 15, 17
Witney blanket 71
wood shavings 45
working cow
   horse 131
worms 175, 176
wounds, first aid
   184–185

Y
Yellow Dun 19

ACKNOWLEDGMENTS

Quarto would like to thank the following agencies, for kindly
supplying images for inclusion in this book:

www.shutterstock.com
www.istockphotos.com

All other images are the copyright of Quarto Publishing plc.
While every effort has been made to credit contributors, Quarto
would like to apologize should there have been any omissions
or errors—and would be pleased to make the appropriate
correction for future editions of the book.

With love to Snoopy.